CB 161 .M87

NAVIGATING THE FUTURE

Books by Bruce C. Murray

THE VIEW FROM SPACE, *with Merton E. Davies*

MARS AND THE MIND OF MAN, *with Arthur C. Clarke, Ray Bradbury, Carl Sagan, and Walter Sullivan*

NAVIGATING
THE FUTURE

BRUCE C. MURRAY

1817

HARPER & ROW, PUBLISHERS

NEW YORK, EVANSTON, SAN FRANCISCO

LONDON

Grateful acknowledgment is hereby made for permission to reprint the following material:

Excerpt on page 150 from "If Only We Had Taller Been" from *When Elephants Last in the Dooryard Bloomed* by Ray Bradbury. Copyright 1973 by Ray Bradbury. Reprinted by permission of Harold Matson Co., Inc.

Excerpt on pages 129–130 from *Intelligent Life in Space* by Frank D. Drake. © Frank D. Drake 1962. Reprinted by permission of Macmillan Publishing Co., Inc.

Excerpt on page 109 from *Nineteen Eighty-four* by George Orwell. Copyright, 1949, by Harcourt Brace Jovanovich, Inc.

Excerpt on pages 127–128 from *The Step to Man* by John R. Platt. Copyright © 1966 by John Wiley & Sons, Inc. Reprinted by permission of John Wiley & Sons, Inc.

Excerpt on page 37 from "Prematurity and Uniqueness in Scientific Discovery" by Gunther S. Stent from *Scientific American*. Copyright © 1972 by Scientific American, Inc.

Excerpt on pages 117–118 from "We Become What We Hate" by William Irwin Thompson. © 1971 by The New York Times Company. Reprinted by permission.

Excerpt on pages 69–70 from *The Shape of Things to Come* by H. G. Wells. Reprinted by permission of the Estate of H. G. Wells.

FIRST EDITION

Designed by Sidney Feinberg

Library of Congress Cataloging in Publication Data

Murray, Bruce C
    Navigating the future.
    Includes bibliographical references.
    1. Forecasting. 2. Civilization, Modern—
1950– I. Title.
CB161.M87 1975   909.82   74–1839
ISBN 0–06–013122–5

75 76 77 78 79 10 9 8 7 6 5 4 3 2 1

THREE DREAMS

The multiple dream like the 40 thieves
Huddled in the cold damp cave
Each dreamer confirming
The collective fantasies
We call reality. . . .
How blinding the visions
Less lonely the nightmares
    Dreaming together.

And the dream of two dreamers
Sharing one dream
Palpable, warm, infinite
For the instant that annihilates space
    And is eaten by time.

The dark unshared dream
Of the solitary dreamer
    That is insanity.

           by CHURCHILL MURRAY
           who has shared his dreams and visions
           of the condition of Man with his son, thereby
           enriching what I have to offer in this book

CONTENTS

FOREWORD

How well did you know your grandfather? I vaguely remember my father's father, who was born in 1863 on the Kentucky frontier, as kindly, old, and very gray. But he speaks out from his unpublished autobiography as a Victorian Romantic I *never* could have understood. My mother's father, born poor in Ireland, spent himself transforming virgin land in central Washington into wheat fields. If miraculously we met now, could he comprehend dimly why (much less how) I have been spending myself exploring barren landscapes of other planets through robot eyes?

Two generations are an enormous interval if measured in units of individual adaptation and reaction to the technological and contemporary social changes of planet Earth.

This cultural foreshortening breeds a pervasive anxiety. Will the world of my grandchildren also be unimaginably different from my own? Will my attitudes and aspirations be comparably obsolete? What has happened to the optimism about the future shared by almost all our grandparents?

I believe we are in the midst of the most rapid and significant period of change in man's history. We of this generation and the next two have the mixed privilege of playing leading roles in a central act of the human drama.

That drama may prove to be a Greek tragedy in which the leading characters were doomed from the start. Who can prove that life is not a cosmic practical joke? Mankind may fail and fall back into a permanent state of barbarism brought on by global nuclear war; or desperate efforts to combat global social disorder and disintegration could lead to a benign failure—the robot societies of *1984* and *Brave New World,* where the individuality has been removed from individuals.

But I *feel,* and choose to believe, that mankind can overcome unprecedented challenges and, in so doing, evolve in culture and in consciousness into a greater species. We will be what we will to be, what we make ourselves worthy of.

This book is about the challenges we face, the possible outcomes of the present, and the profound implications for human values represented by those choices.

Such an ambitious scope tends to make a physical scientist feel vulnerable, accustomed as he is to constructing his intellectual edifices within his "expert" territory, buttressed by observational evidence. The reader will recognize immediately what I have only slowly learned to accept. This work is a personal one; its author cannot remain completely protected behind the shield of scholarship and expert opinion.

This endeavor did not begin as a monologue. To sharpen my focus, to identify the topics and issues of greatest interest, I entered into broad-ranging dialogues comparing my thoughts and concerns with those of eight very different men, each of unusual accomplishment and perception. Their words show up scattered here and there in the text, but my intellectual debt is much greater.

Three of the eight are close colleagues at Caltech, all distinguished scientists. Harrison Brown, a chemist and geochemist of world-wide renown, has for many years been in the forefront of population and resource studies. He was Foreign Secretary of the United States National Academy of Sciences from 1968 to 1974.

Robert Sinsheimer is a biologist, Chairman of the Division of Biological Sciences at Caltech, and especially concerned with the possibilities of genetic engineering.

Murray Gell-Mann is a Nobel laureate in Physics, a celebrated theoretician, and a man of omnivorous intellectual appetite. He served on the President's Science Advisory Council (PSAC) before President Nixon in 1972 abolished that unique nonpartisan source of competent advice.

Another scientist with great understanding both of science and of its interaction with government in America is Gordon MacDonald, a distinguished environmentalist and former member of the Environmental Quality Council of the United States. He also served on President Johnson's PSAC.

Since there are more dimensions to reality than those embraced directly by physical science, I sought opinions and attitudes of some whose professional interests are more directly concerned with the subjective side of man. Professor Robert Nisbet is one of the most highly respected sociologists and historians in the United States.

Judge David Bazelon is on the front line of law and justice as Chief Judge of the Circuit Court of Appeals of the Washington, D.C., district. He has been known as a liberal judge, although such labels are sometimes misleading.

Senator John Tunney deals daily with the problems of the nation in Congress. I have come to know him as a thoughtful, perceptive individual.

And though I am not absorbed by organized religion myself, it warrants the most serious consideration in postulating future realities for mankind. One modern theologian with whom I enjoy discussion of the two worlds of science and theology is Morton Kelsey, an Episcopal priest on the faculty of Notre Dame (happy evidence of the ecumenical movement).

I wish to express my gratitude to all eight, as well as to others who are listed on page 174.

Come, let us share facts and opinions of the present, "blinding visions" and "lonely nightmares," viewing them as clues to the "collective fantasies" of our descendants. Perhaps we may sense the possibility of a future reality big enough for both the feelings of men and the facts of science, for both the natural and the artificial, for both our grandparents and our grandchildren.

BRUCE MURRAY

Pasadena, California
December, 1974

NAVIGATING THE FUTURE

I

QUEST FOR PERSPECTIVE

*

48 Woodstock Road
Oxford
8 October 1914

To the Council of the University of Birmingham

GENTLEMEN,

I beg to apply for the Poynting Professorship of Physics. I enclose particulars of my qualifications, copies of my scientific papers and testimonials from Sir Ernest Rutherford, Prof. J. S. Townsend and Prof. W. H. Bragg. . . . I have been nominated for and hope to obtain a temporary commission in the regular army preferably in the Royal Engineers. My services are not therefore likely to be available while the war lasts.

I am,

Your obedient servant,
H. G. J. MOSELEY (1887–1915)[1]

ENDING OR BEGINNING?

As the year A.D. 1000 approached, there was a widespread belief in Europe that the world would end precisely at dawn of the first day of the first year of the millennium. Thousands awaited the dawn on hilltops, dressed in their Sunday best, having given away their homes and worldly possessions as proof of their faith.

Nine hundred years later, the Western world had achieved smug complacency about the future and pride

1

in the present as the best of all possible civilizations. Articles of Faith included the superiority of the white man and his destiny to rule "lesser breeds"; the convictions that his way of living and dressing should be adopted by all decent people, that the increase in manufactured products was the road to human freedom and happiness as well as to higher dividends, that the natural was vulgar and ugly but the artificial elegant and desirable.

In the world of 1900, man felt confident he had learned the basic secrets of nature. All the great mysteries had been solved; the universe, many thought, was as easy to understand as a giant machine.

Everything was in its place, neatly tagged. Matter consisted of "hard glassy particles" (as Newton described them) that could never be destroyed or altered. (Soon a young man named Einstein would announce a formula that made matter vanish into energy, but which few would care about . . . until Hiroshima.)

In 1900, after nearly a hundred years of relative peace, there was a widespread belief that a great war was no longer likely in the modern world. Even in 1914, and later in 1939, few could believe that millions would perish in a world-wide holocaust as ancient empires clashed and vanished and dictators rose from obscurity, willing to destroy entire races to achieve their ambitions. Our world today is the product of those two world wars that ended man's smugness about world peace and brought our very survival into question.

The year 1973 marked the five-hundredth anniversary of the birth of Copernicus, leader of the Western world's first great scientific revolution, which displaced Earth from the center of the solar system in man's cosmogony and initiated an intellectual explosion. Half a millennium of science, its applications and implications, have completely changed the face of Earth, overwhelmed man's mind, and left his spirit adrift.

In a remarkable, if unconscious, commemoration of the Copernicus cinquecentennial, Earth fired off seven sky-rockets toward those same planets whose motions first led man to recognize rational patterns in God's handiwork.

A slowly spinning automatic spacecraft, Pioneer 10, carried out man's first close-up inspection of giant Jupiter, our dominant planet. It carries on its carefully machined body a polished plaque with cryptic symbols intended for alien eyes; for Jupiter's enormous gravity will fling it completely out of our solar system. One does not know just where in interstellar space, and when, it may encounter something unexpected. An identical twin, Pioneer 11, followed a year behind, targeted toward Saturn after its encounter with Jupiter.

Four large Russian spacecraft reached Mars; their objective was to land two scientific stations on the surface and, through television eyes, let man see for the first time a surface-oriented view of the red planet, bringing to a climax the long romance between Mars and the Mind of Man.[2] But Soviet efforts to explore Mars seem jinxed; the landings were unsuccessful and that close-up view of the surface will have to await later flights.

Streaking in toward the Sun, rather than away from it, the U.S. probe Mariner 10 trained its television eyes on the clouds of Venus before being flung inward still farther, toward the blistering region of the mysterious planet Mercury. There those telescopic television eyes provided thousands of pictures of that completely unexplored planet.

And as though God himself wished to join the commemoration, a new comet, a natural space probe, sped right through the midst of all this interplanetary activity.

This is a remarkable time for space exploration, and especially for the few, like myself, who participate directly in such unprecedented enterprises. Space exploration has been a mind-expanding experience for mankind as the other worlds of our solar system have become for the first time real—if not familiar.

But the close-up appearance of planet Earth is not so elevating or exhilarating. Man finds himself on a planet polluted by his material progress, being made uninhabitable by his fertility, and threatened with annihilation by his modern weapons. It is difficult to ignore man and his terrestrial predicament even as I explore distant planets.

IS THE PRESENT UNPRECEDENTED?

Can the past be a valid guide for the future? Or are we living in a period without precedent in history? Are we near the end of an epoch, perhaps even the end of Western civilization? Or is history somehow replaying itself in modern electronic and plastic form but with the substance of human existence unchanged?

If the present is unprecedented, then where shall we find the strength and wisdom to meet the difficulties, uncertainties, and seemingly senseless violence and disorder that threaten to engulf us? What frame of reference can we use to determine present morality if previous morality seems less and less applicable to modern dilemmas?

Margaret Mead says we have only twenty-five years to solve mankind's problems or else.[3] Unprecedented ecological catastrophe is forecast by Jacques Cousteau[4] and Paul Ehrlich.[5] If the comments of these and many others are any indication, then surely mankind is in an unprecedented period of history.

Thoughtful scholars I know personally agree independently with my own assessment: mankind is today experiencing circumstances for which there is no adequate historical parallel.[6] But individuals tend to call attention to *different* aspects of the current scene. Mankind is in such an unprecedented period that its manifestations appear everywhere.

For example, environmentalist Gordon MacDonald comments:

> We are going through an unprecedented period of technological change. New possibilities for technology are continuing to increase. I suspect one of the major differences between past experience and the present is the recognition by many that we have to evaluate what these changes mean in the long term for society. In the past it's been assumed that if you made a technical advance something good was to come out of it. It increased your scientific knowledge and understanding. This by itself would lead to an improvement in the well-being of mankind. Many people are beginning to question that. Frankly, I've started to question it myself.

Geochemist Harrison Brown believes that:

> In a very real sense history is being repeated, but with a difference. . . . In a remarkably short period of time human society has literally fissioned into two cultures which we can call the culture of the rich and the culture of the poor. Now we always had rich people and we always had poor people, but in the last twenty years a complete bimodality has emerged with almost nothing in between.

Physicist Murray Gell-Mann comments that:

> Human interference with the world is reaching a point of a hundred percent perturbation rather than a small perturbation. Man's unprecedented effects are noticeable on the environment, the physical and nonhuman life of the planet, on individuals and their capacity for dealing with other individuals, and finally on society itself. Prior to becoming such a

major perturbation on this planet, we were not controlling evolution, our own or other people's, and social groupings arose fairly naturally.

Biologist Robert Sinsheimer chooses four examples to illustrate that the present is unprecedented:

First, unlimited warfare is clearly no longer an acceptable means for the resolution of human differences. Second, we are coming close to the saturation level of the planet as far as human existence is concerned. Third, the possibilities of extensive prolongation of life cause the whole concept of unconditional preservation of life to become complex and unprecedented. Fourth is the possibility of rather massive intervention in what will be necessarily a limited human population in the gene pool as well as the unprecedented conceivable ability to create wholly new genes which might advance Man beyond anything known.

Sociologist Robert Nisbet emphasizes:

I can see apparent signs of a protective apathy already coming over large numbers of us in Western society. There is a seeming failure of the federal government to solve domestic problems. I think that apparent failure has become sufficiently believed now by the controlling elites in this country to lead almost certainly to some kind of significant reaction to it. . . . What we know least about as a result of thousands of years of civilized history is affluence. We are the first affluent state, politically, psychologically, and sociologically. And yet there is something about affluence that does not seem to produce community. Poverty will produce community—a sense of spirit, of organization, of working together. Affluence doesn't seem to.

Judge David Bazelon has pointed out:

People are getting away from the idea that this is the way it's supposed to be. This is how the guy figured it out upstairs and there's no use arguing with him. People are beginning more and more to see that they don't have to take the dirty end of the stick and that there is a chance to do something about it. I can't say that in earlier times people weren't also aware of injustice and oppression, but now the business of accepting it has changed.

I had expected that Senator John Tunney might develop the possibility of the obsolescence of political institutions or the political process. Instead, he deals with a much more general problem:

The religiosity of the medieval period is in this century dying to the point that it now is really a shell of what existed. When man lost the sense of fear that his actions were being judged by an Almighty that was within himself and outside himself, man developed situation ethics, which simply means that he could choose his ethical and moral standards dependent upon the pressures of any one moment in time.

Finally, theologian Morton Kelsey feels that there is a

... change in the philosophy of science, which is moving from a cocksure positivism to a much more open-ended view of reality. Once this is achieved, then religious experience is not something necessarily kooky. I rather suspect that we may have to have a time of confusion and chaos before modern man will take seriously the implications of the philosophy of science and take seriously the inner world of man, the non-physical dimension of reality.

The past does not entirely carry the key to the future; there is a new element. The last fifty years may have as much to do with the future as the previous five hundred.

THE FUTURE OF FUTUROLOGY

During the last decade an entire business of peering into the future has developed as part of the information industry, although its success so far in predicting even short intervals of future is not spectacular. One of the best known "futurists," Herman Kahn, achieved international stature while at Rand, studying there the implications of nuclear war. His book *On Thermonuclear War*[7] examined possible scenarios of thermonuclear war in sufficient detail to cause alarm and consternation among both government officials and the public. The picture he painted of the implications of nuclear war for either the so-called victors or vanquished was sufficiently disquieting to have exerted some restraint on the United States in actions from which nuclear war was a possible outcome. More recently, elaborate computer modeling of resource/population/energy/environmental crises such as are described in *The Limits to Growth*[8] have become fashionable. The first true treatise on "the post-industrial society" was published in 1973 by Daniel Bell.[9]

Herman Kahn founded one of the first of the major organizations to concentrate on the future, Hudson Institute, to expand his predictive capability beyond the confines of nuclear war and the Rand Corporation. In 1967 Kahn produced a major predictive effort entitled *The Year 2000*.[10] Yet an articulate critic of the "mindless liberal technocratic managerial vision," William Irwin Thompson, has singled out Kahn's book as an illustration of the inadequacy of quantitative prediction:

> . . . none of the problems that come up in *The Limits to Growth* are even in Herman Kahn's book. . . . You would

imagine he would be able to be at least five years in advance of himself.... Not a thing about pollution. Already it's ancient history.[11]

As we shall see in Chapter III, geochemist Brown and others concerned with forecasts of population and food supplies have also found their estimates outmoded within only six or seven years.

One of the few humorous articles by Harrison Brown I have come across is a parable for futurists entitled "Herman Cohn in Retrospect,"[12] in which he pokes gentle humor at Herman Kahn by developing the character of Herman Cohn, supposedly a science consultant to William Jennings Bryan during his 1908 campaign. Cohn "was confident that one day he would become chairman of the President's Science Advisory Committee," and had been hired by Bryan because of a misunderstanding which might well have resulted from poor hearing. When asked by Bryan whether he was a fundamentalist, Cohn had replied, "Yes, I am fundamental," and he was hired. Brown purports to have found some of the unpublished manuscripts from 1908 of this forgotten futurist, entitled "On Nitroglycerin War," "The Decline and Fall of British and French Empires," "The Coming Russian Superstate," and "Will Railroads Become Obsolete?" none of which was accepted for publication. He then continues his parody with Cohn's pessimistic prediction of the effects of the internal combustion engine:

> Herman Cohn alone forecast trouble. "I agree," he said, "that it would be pleasant to walk on streets free of animal waste products. But can we be sure that the waste products of the automobile will be an improvement?"

This hypothetical figure, Cohn, felt to the end of his life that our political leaders of the cities, county, state and national levels are intelligent and practical persons who know how to get things done. Thus far their work has been confined almost entirely to the solution of critical current problems. It seems clear that they must now begin to devote time and energy to the solution of problems *before they actually become problems.* I am confident that once our leaders read these forecasts they will take action which is designed to forestall the predicted end result.

Are we really helpless captives between an irrelevant past and an obscure future? I think not. It is impossible to predict the precise course of events, but it is extremely useful to consider the range of possible outcomes. Indeed, to me this is the most significant aspect of future studies. Just as we have been challenged either to understand our past or to repeat it, so must we comprehend the full range of future possibilities if we are not to act out the worst of them. We must view ourselves in a perspective that includes both the past and future if the present is to have meaning—if we are to understand where we are going and why our fate is worth the cost and struggle.

II

SCIENCE AND THE MIND OF MAN

*

In the dust, where we have buried
The silent races and their abominations,
We have buried so much of the delicate magic of life.

D. H. LAWRENCE[1]

W HO ARE WE? We are those who lived before us and those who will live afterward, sharing a cosmic lifetime. We were not created instantly at birth; we began to be in a momentous event more than three billion years ago when the first self-replicating molecule formed by chance. We will not entirely die so long as our thoughts, our imaginative creations, persist faintly within the consciousness of distant descendants and their cultures.

The Present is constructed from the successes and failures of the Past. As the pace of man's activity accelerated, the variety of consciousness and cultures from different eras telescoped together. Thus there are diverse realities. "Mankind" is many groups of men with differing impressions of reality limited by their senses and imaginations, like blind men trying to describe an unseen elephant that they can investigate only by touch.

Primitive people were discovered recently in the Philippines who have been isolated since before the arrival there of Europeans, perhaps much longer.[2] They are truly living fossils, cultural fossils. Of the countries represented in the United Nations, how many are there whose populations really believe that stars seen at night are actually other suns? Yet within the two most powerful nations, leading scientists aspire to communicate by radio with the possible inhabitants of planets circling some of those other suns.

As the year 2000 approaches, the governments of the world still include absolute monarchies; even the practice of the primitive punishment of mutilation survives in isolated cases. Most of the world's inhabitants still have little voice in determining their future, even while immense revolutionary experiments struggle vainly in pursuit of "From each according to his ability, to each according to his needs."[3]

Perhaps half the people who ever lived are alive today, and they are truly children of the Space Age, since almost half are less than twenty years old. Yet echoes of most of the cultural patterns that ever existed resound faintly within the intricately confused diversity that constitutes modern consciousness. This amalgam of perceptions of reality, and of beliefs concerning right and wrong, will have a profound influence on the events of the future and on the consciousness of future men.

THE GEOLOGIST'S VIEW

First let us consider the long-range view, that of the geologist, who sees mankind on a cosmic time scale. To him, man is one of the most recently developed animals in a biological evolution of over three billion years.

One of the most striking aspects of mankind is the brevity of time the species has been on Earth. If the duration of life on Earth were regarded as a "cosmic" year, then man was born only a few hours before midnight, December 31. An alternative unit of time for such com-

parisons is the generation, the interval which limits genetic as well as environmentally controlled change.
Geologist William Schopf of UCLA has observed recently:

> The number of generations since the beginning are stag-
> gering for some living systems compared with man. These
> systems have had tremendous opportunities to develop new
> versions of their life form. Bacteria for example have been
> through 10 trillion generations, some shelled sea creatures
> through 60 million, horses 27 million, and elephants 10 mil-
> lion. By contrast, man, who is one of the most recent evolu-
> tionary innovations, has so far only benefited from the im-
> provements possible over 200 thousand generations.[4]

Bringing this time scale up to the present, there have
been less than 800 generations since the end of the last Ice
Age, perhaps only 350 since the rise of what we term
civilization in the Middle East. Most Americans are separated by less than ten generations from the signing of the
Declaration of Independence.[5] Man as a distinct primate
genus is geologically young. Man as the social, intelligent
being we consider ourselves to be has existed but a moment on the panorama of geological and biological evolution.

Man is a creature of the Ice Ages, which are rare and
unusual occurrences in the history of this planet. The
oldest fossils now considered to be of the same genus as
man are between two and three million years old.[6] The
human time scale thus approximates that of the present
episode of Ice Ages, termed the *Pleistocene* Period.

Is Another Ice Age Due?

Only two earlier Ice Ages on Earth have been recorded,
separated by unequal intervals of hundreds of millions of

years. The cause of these anomalous coolings of the Earth and formations of permanent ice over significant fractions of its surface has challenged scientific imagination for nearly a century.

Since the end of World War II and the peacetime application of nuclear chemistry, natural radioactive clocks have been used to date the alternations between the cold and temperate conditions that characterize the present Ice Age episode. There are many environmental manifestations of the waxing and waning of Ice Ages: sea-level fluctuation, changes in the temperature of the sea as well as the air, deposition of characteristic deposits of dust and debris, depression and gradual rebound of glacially covered areas. Variations of air temperature are recorded in Greenland glacial ice, of ocean temperature in the sediments of the gulf of the Caribbean, of forest changes in loess and clay deposits in Czechoslovakia, of vegetation in peat bogs in Greece, and of sea level in a sequence of corals preserved on Barbados Island in the Caribbean.

Such studies consistently point toward a sudden warming eleven thousand years ago (preceding the first development of agriculture) and also indicate previous fluctuations in climate of from tens to hundreds of thousands years' duration. At least one well-regarded expert thinks a return to cold conditions may be due for the Earth within the next hundred to a thousand years.[7] Such a return would obviously have a disastrous impact on agriculture, adding to the calamity of unrestricted population growth.

And there are shorter-term fluctuations in climate as well (of from tens to hundreds of years) that have affected man's past and present. Hannibal's crossing of the Alps to attack Rome apparently came near the end of a warm period. The return of colder conditions caused glaciers to block the strategic mountain passes once again, thereby shielding Rome for several centuries from an associated southward migration of "barbarian" tribes.[8] Similarly, a slight global cooling trend may be responsible for the present sub-Saharan drought and accompanying hunger and deprivation there.[9]

Just as man's primate genetic makeup is the product of selective adaptation to continued climatic and other environmental changes over tens of millions of years, so man's social and cultural evolution has been dominated by the necessity to adapt successfully to climatic changes on a scale much too short for successful biological evolution.

Man is truly a creature of the Ice Ages, surviving them thus far through his unique intellectual and social abilities to modify his environment and to accumulate and transmit knowledge and experience.

Man and Natural Cataclysms

Furthermore, the very ground we stand on is moving. Continents continue to change their positions. The huge plates that make up the Earth's crust adjust themselves on occasion with a trembling spasm. The famous, or notorious (depending on one's point of view), San Andreas Fault of California is the boundary of two of these plates and seems both now and in the past to have been moving at geologically phenomenal rates, several inches per year on the average. Within the last thirty million years, parts of what is now California have been displaced northward at least three hundred miles.[10] Local rates of deformation are also significant. For example, the Baldwin Hills area within urban Los Angeles is rising at an average of 1-1/2 to 2-1/2 feet per century as a result of intermittent fault activity.[11]

Earthquakes, sometimes accompanied by devastating

seismic sea waves, are the normal geological means by which the Earth relieves its strains and accomplishes differential motion. Earthquakes are common enough in parts of California to require the application of a certain amount of preventive engineering in order to lessen potential damage. The design and construction of large buildings, dams, and nuclear power plants have been markedly affected. Even more restrictive policies are now going into practice.

Elsewhere in the continental United States, however, building construction rarely reflects concern for potential earthquakes since they are not frequent enough to receive priority in local and state government. Yet one of the largest earthquakes ever recorded occurred in 1811 in New Madrid, in the wilderness of what is now Missouri.[12] Were similar shaking to take place in this area today, the damage and loss of life would be immense because of the brick construction still widespread there, even greater than the potential toll from a similar quake in California.

In some earthquake-prone underdeveloped nations, the geologically inevitable is disregarded more flagrantly. Managua, Nicaragua, was damaged by severe shocks in 1885, 1931, and 1968. Yet the population grew from 56,000 in 1940 to 420,000 by the time the devastating shock of December 23, 1973, struck. Five thousand persons died, in part due to the breakdown of governmental functions. Half a billion dollars in property damage was sustained, an average per capita loss of about $1,000. By comparison, the stronger San Fernando, California, earthquake of February 9, 1972, killed only sixty, even though the total property damage was comparable. Also, since the damage was absorbed financially in part by a much larger and cohesive political unit (Los Angeles County), the per capita property loss was only about $70.[13] Even nature charges higher prices to the poor.

Natural catastrophes are commonplace and recurrent phenomena. Earthquakes and explosive volcanic eruptions such as Krakatoa, Mount Pelée, or the enormous explosion that shook the eastern Mediterranean around 1500 B.C. (at what is now the island of Thera) are part of a broad spectrum of "cataclysms." As the human species multiplied to occupy more and more areas of the Earth's surface, it became increasingly vulnerable to natural catastrophe. For example, in November, 1970, a rather normal storm situation in the Bay of Bengal took a slightly abnormal turn, resulting in the flooding of a large area of the coast of what is now Bangladesh. Around 500,000 helpless people were drowned,[14] yet the world hardly noticed. This storm situation would not have been classified by scientists even as anomalous, since it is a rather common occurrence there.

So long as man continues his present behavior, death and material loss from natural catastrophe will hardly compete with his own capacity for self-destruction. However, as population growth inevitably slows, and the once seemingly inexhaustible supply of natural resources becomes more limited, natural catastrophe may conceivably return to the prominence it once held in early civilizations. The final blow to a brilliant culture was often unrecoverable damage from earthquake, seismic sea wave, or volcanic explosion, if not the slower starvation brought about by climatic change.

Man, the Colonial Organism

A final aspect of the geologist's view is man's growing dependence upon greater numbers of his own species for survival. Primitive man lived in small tribal units scattered widely with low population density, agricultural man in family units in small communities. Modern man lives in crowded cities, wholly dependent on the services of thousands of others whom he never sees and never knows. Through social evolution he is developing truly into what the geologist describes as a colonial organism, like coral. The cultural heritage of primitive man one day will finally become extinct, and then man will have lost forever the capability for independent survival. He will have completed an evolutionary step just as profound as if he had evolved genetically into a morphologically different species.

THE PERSISTENT PAST

Changes in man's way of life have led to changes in his consciousness. Indeed, it is his very consciousness that sets man apart from other animals—he can contemplate himself. Or, as Julian Huxley puts it, ". . . in modern scientific man, evolution was at last contemplating itself."[15] It was this consciousness of himself, with its attendant ability to reason, which enabled man to survive against larger and more powerful enemies until he became literally the lord of all living things.

To trace carefully and completely the evolution of consciousness from the primitive to the present is a task which would dwarf even Will Durant's ten-volume *Story of Civilization*.[16] Rather, I wish to highlight my own view of the myriad past consciousnesses which still persist today, albeit in distorted and blended form. Our modern dilemmas of value derive from that very diversity of perceptions of reality. Therefore we must view ourselves in the context of our persistent past in order to find a broader framework in which dilemma and paradox can at least be bypassed, if not resolved.

Primitive Consciousness

Judging from the archaeological record, genus *Homo* seems to have developed a state of consciousness which included religious belief and artistic representation of nature only within the last 100,000 years. The magnificent cave paintings in France and Spain are evidently not more than 30,000 years old. The earliest evidence of a lunar calendar (and probably worship) may be regular markings which were carved on a reindeer antler only 1500 generations ago.

Evolution is not necessarily progressive or direct. Thus the fact that twentieth-century man is the latest in the sequence of man, conscious man, does not necessarily mean his consciousness is broader and "better" in every way than that of his predecessors, or even includes the essential elements of primitive consciousness, for example. Indeed, it is difficult to know confidently whether or not primitive consciousness contains some important insights about reality which may have been lost or distorted by rational Western culture.

Laurens Van Der Post, who described the search for unspoiled human survivors from the past among the South African Bushmen in *The Lost World of the Kalahari*,[17] and his impressions of their myths and consciousness in *The Heart of the Hunter*,[18] feels that primitive consciousness may partake of a harmony between man and nature that modern man has lost.

Theologian Morton Kelsey has nicely summarized the primitive awareness of what we would term nonphysical reality:

> All of these cultures manifest the belief that, beside the physical world, there is another significant world of reality

that breaks in upon the individual, particularly in dreams
. . . this idea occurs among peoples everywhere, except in
modern Western culture, where it is so foreign that men find
it difficult to comprehend. It persists among modern primitive peoples, as [demonstrated by] dream experiences among
Bantus, Ashantis, Navajos, Papuans, and others. Jung found
the same thing when he visited the Hopi Indians and certain
African tribes to study their dream experiences. . . . Among
peoples who have not been touched by Western positivism
there is an almost universal belief that man is in contact
through dreams with something more substantial than his
own imaginings.[19]

In primitive consciousness it was literally a magical
world. Everything in the physical world had a life of its
own. Nature represented the symbolism of the world of
spirit. This perception of reality preceded modern man's
evolution to his present state and still lingers even among
"modern" peoples in the form of superstitions and the
acceptance of astrology and the occult, for example.

Civilization and the Mind of Man

Primitive man felt part of his environment. The forests
were not lumber to cut down nor an obstruction to clear
away. They were the source of his sustenance: meat and
fruits and wild vegetables. Only slowly did he conceive
the idea of changing nature and bending it to his will.
Finally, seven to eight thousand years ago, the revolutionary ideas developed of planting wild seeds instead of
searching for native plants, and of taming and multiplying
wild animals and fowl instead of hunting them.
The world's first population explosion followed, and
unprecedented feats of art, architecture, and engineering were accomplished. Primitive cultures, politically

egalitarian from economic necessity, began to be replaced by the despotic regimes of the ancient civilizations, exploiting the revolutionary economic concepts of division of labor and taxation.

On the Mediterranean periphery of the great kingdoms of ancient times some who remained unconquered were moving in a new direction. In early Greece the world witnessed the first stirrings of free inquiry into the nature of man and the universe. A new and audacious idea developed in the mind of man, an idea that, despite long nights of barbarism, was to be reborn again and again. Man was *free* to try to understand reality and fulfill his individual potential. Unlike the Egyptians with their mummies and pyramids, the Greeks were concerned with life and not with death. Humanity was glorified. The human body was honored in art and literature for strength and beauty, and not so much for the rank of the person. Perhaps the greatest contribution of Greek civilization to our world and to the world of the future was the concept of reason and logic as the means to confirm truth. Euclid's geometry with its meticulous proofs was a necessary preconditioning for science. The Greeks left a rich and articulate literature of their discoveries in science and mathematics as well as their philosophies and speculations on the nature of reality.

The Rise of Rationalism

The philosophical schism initiated by the speculations of Plato and Aristotle remains an important attribute of the diversity of Western consciousness. Plato argued for a dualistic world which included elements of reality beyond the powers of knowledge perceived directly through the senses. Aristotle attempted to restrict all knowledge to that which can be derived through the senses or by the power of deductive reasoning. The early Christian Church carried along Platonic ideas.[20] Religious healing and the miraculous interpretation of dreams and visions prevailed almost without challenge until the delayed arrival of the works of Aristotle impacted Western theological thinking.

Thomas Aquinas brought about a new rationalization of Christianity to reduce its dependence upon a *continuing* spiritual intervention in the lives of men. Yet the Roman Catholic Church still continues to require evidence of miracles for canonization. The idea of direct communication with God by means of dreams or visions and "being saved" has also been a strong continuing trend within Protestant sects, which look to the Old Testament for authority.

The seeds of Aristotle took hold and grew vigorously in the fervent Renaissance. Science became formally established by Copernicus, Kepler, and Galileo, followed by Descartes, Newton, and Leibnitz.

Traditional views inherited from the classical world clashed with the newer views of science, reaching a climax with Darwin and the idea of biological evolution. Man himself, it was argued, is descended from other animals. Where now was the special divinity of man?

Misunderstanding of science led some in the nineteenth century to the view that science itself could provide a new basis for human values. Thus was born scientific materialism. It was argued that everything we think or experience as human beings is derived from our senses. Values and mores are nothing more than inherited social patterns without objective meaning. Indeed, T. H. Huxley, the great propagandist for Darwin's views, is credited with inventing the term "agnostic."

Scientific materialism became popular among some

educated people in the Western world during the last hundred years and extended even into the political and economic arena in the form of Marxism, the variety of socialism which has obtained greatest currency in our world.

The Obsolescence of Mechanism

Meanwhile physics outgrew its absolute mechanistic adolescence to recognize a strange new reality in which clocks and hearts beat more slowly the faster we move. Even matter, "this too too solid flesh," befuddled our intuition by demonstrating wave properties, like the grin of the vanishing Cheshire cat, yet remaining as real as diffracted electrons. "Elementary" particles have proven to be composite, one level of structure of a subatomic world in which a series of shells seemingly enclose one another —like an endless Chinese puzzle.

And while "objective" behavioral biology and psychology have observed relentlessly the exterior of the human mind and personality, the intuitive and partly subjective approach of Freud, Adler, and Jung and their followers seems to provide a little insight into the subtle complexities of ourselves. Significantly, Jung concluded:

> I should like to call attention to the following facts: during the past thirty years, people from all the civilized countries of the Earth have consulted me. . . . Among all my patients in the second half of life—this is to say, over thirty-five, there has not been one whose problem in the last resort was not that of finding a religious outlook on life.[21]

Mechanistic science proved to be inadequate even as a description of twentieth-century physical reality, much less as a basis for understanding the psyche. Nevertheless, scientific materialism has challenged traditional concepts of reality and value throughout man's domain, leaving a trail of confusion, isolation, and spiritual anguish. I think the *implications* of science have been even more devastating than its *applications*. Thus we must understand carefully the limits of science in order to place it in a broader intellectual framework.

THE LIMITS OF SCIENCE

Science and especially its philosophical brother-in-law, scientific materialism, have dominated intellectual thought for more than a century. The methods and concepts of physical science have been carried well beyond the realm of physical phenomena into such diverse fields as human behavior, economics, and politics. It is important to remember, therefore, that science can deal only with what is observable and, further, only with the reproducible, or at least the recurrent.[22] It is powerless to form an authoritative opinion on transitory or problematical phenomena (so long as those phenomena remain so), a drawback in earlier times to the acceptance, for example, of ball lightning, the aurora borealis, the living coelacanth, Freudian psychology, and lunar impact cratering.

UFO's, Science, and Reality

The limits of science are highlighted by the continuing debate over UFO's—Unidentified Flying Objects. To some scientists, reports of flashing lights in the sky at night, and even of saucer-like objects with humanoid shapes involved, are so preposterous that they offend their sense of what ought to be rational and, therefore, what ought to be nature. Harvard astronomy professor

Donald Menzel attempted to explain away all reported UFO phenomena as common things in uncommon circumstances—for example, high-flying balloons, or Venus in the twilight sky.[23] For him there was no possibility that unknown physical phenomena really were involved in even a fraction of the reports. A later study sponsored by the National Academy of Sciences came to a similar conclusion—that "Careful consideration of the record as it is available to us leads us to conclude that further extensive study of UFO's probably cannot be justified in the expectation that science will be advanced thereby."[24] In effect these studies said: Not only are UFO's improbable, but they should not be studied further!

The Soviet Union is also officially studying the UFO problem under the auspices of the "Committee for Contact with Extraterrestrial Intelligence."[25] The title alone suggests that UFO's may fare better in Russia than in the United States.

Diametrically opposed to the dogmatic, negative point of view are those who have become entranced with the reports. They not only acknowledge the existence of new phenomena but feel compelled to infer a bizarre explanation—extraterrestrial intelligent activity. The late Professor James E. McDonald of the University of Arizona seemed to have fallen into this class, reminiscent of Percival Lowell and his obsession with the possibility of intelligent life on Mars.

To me, both kinds of reactions are unscientific.[26] There simply are not enough hard data to argue scientifically that an unrecognizable transient object in the sky is or is not something presently unknown to science—either a minor thing or maybe even an extraordinary thing. One may develop a strong intuition about the matter, but still on a subjective basis.

Extrasensory perception (ESP) and certain related purported phenomena, passionately believed in by a small group of advocates, are generally ignored by the main body of science as too preposterous to warrant consideration. However, ESP is receiving renewed scientific study, even with minor federal support.[27] Both UFO's and ESP at the present time are not within the realm of science because they have not met the criteria of being reproducible or at least recurrent,[28] for other than a tiny minority of scientists. They may never meet those criteria for a sufficiently large number of scientists to become accepted. Or new convincing observations could conceivably come about to bring acceptance. Or existing facts might later become meaningful in the context of a new scientific view.

Trans-science and Radiation Hazards

The limits of science can be misunderstood not only by the public but by scientists themselves. Physicist Alvin Weinberg has coined the term "trans-science" to describe extensions of scientific reality where there simply are not enough statistics to go on.[29] There have not been enough occurrences, nor can the specific situation be reproduced in a laboratory. Yet the question still pertains to physical reality. As examples of trans-science, he cites the difficulties in assessing reactor safety and low-level-radiation hazard.

There never has been a major reactor accident, and therefore it is difficult to estimate the probability of one occurring. Similarly, it is difficult to estimate the effects of very low-level radiation on biological samples because there simply has not been enough time, nor enough specimens, to acquire valid statistics. Yet both problems are of great and continuing public concern. Thus there is scientific uncertainty about the outcome of a real situation with very great human implications. Is the human genetic makeup threatened by the use of nuclear energy? How does one deal with this sort of problem? Trans-science is a very important concept to a world desperately trying to be the master and not the slave of technology, a world struggling to find human values in the jungle of numbers and abstractions that pervade modern living.

Another dramatic example of trans-science was acted out in the late fifties and early sixties. Two eminent scientists, Linus Pauling and Edmund Teller, led opposing political campaigns concerning atmospheric nuclear testing. Pauling wanted to outlaw nuclear testing, Teller to make it more acceptable.

In fact, neither man dealt with the problem within the strict realm of science. Neither had at his disposal accurate statistics concerning the probable human cost of nuclear fallout. The geochemical processes that concentrate or disperse harmful isotopes had not yet been unraveled sufficiently, nor were the actual biological effects within the body known accurately. Both, in effect, were using their scientific prestige to reinforce a political point of view. Pauling, I believe, felt that nuclear war must be avoided at all costs and that weapons testing increased the likelihood of weapons use. Teller, on the other hand, I believe, felt that an early, decisive confrontation with the Soviets might not necessarily be a bad thing in the long run of history. The members of the Nobel Committee tended to agree with Pauling, so he received a Nobel Peace Prize (to complement an earlier prize in chemistry) for this excursion into trans-science and politics.

At an even earlier epoch in the development of nuclear energy, trans-science had been encountered within the scientific group that developed the first atomic bomb (exploded as a test in New Mexico in 1945). There was some concern that this first fission reaction might trigger an uncontrolled reaction in Earth's atmosphere itself, thereby obliterating the world. This was deemed an unlikely, but nevertheless finite, possibility at the time. According to one biographical account, this prospect was assessed to be one or two chances in a million. That risk was deemed acceptable (an interesting problem in value); but I doubt very much that it was possible to assess the odds at all confidently. Probably then, as in so many other cases, scientists relied on their intuition and "guesstimates" to deal with problems for which they simply didn't have an adequate factual basis. They were better qualified to guess the odds than the political and military authorities—but that was all.

Trans-science and Space Exploration

The tiresome debate over the last decade and a half concerning the extent to which unmanned vehicles need to be sterilized before landing on Mars is a similar exercise in trans-science. Since the value, albeit negative, of contaminating the previously pristine planetary biology with terrestrial organisms is large, the probability of doing so should be made small. However, if it is quite uncertain whether life is there at all, then carrying these precepts in a mathematical form leads to an absurdity. Indeed, in my opinion that is what has happened to U.S. efforts in the sterilization of spacecraft.[30] Scientific "guesstimates" and intuition concerning the likelihood of life on Mars are quite subjective (including my own) and easily colored by the scientist's subjective judgment of the value of protecting any pristine Martian biology.

The widely publicized "sterile" handling of the lunar samples returned by Apollo 11 was not only an example of trans-science but a questionable exercise in public relations. Virtually none of the scientists involved expected any lunar biology, much less a toxic one. Yet the probability of release of those samples through an accident during entry or recovery was quite real. Had there been *any* real biological hazard, then it was quite irresponsible to attempt the return of samples at all. If the hazard was insignificant, then the men-in-white-coats scene at Houston was little more than show.

Unwarranted publicizing of hypothetical lunar and Martian biology by early NASA officials may have created an irrational legacy for future NASA management. They will be faced with the unwanted offspring of an illicit affair between public relations and trans-science. This is because space planners now are considering the feasibility of the return of a sample of *Mars* to Earth (with unmanned spacecraft, perhaps in the 1980's). But the specter of the contamination of Earth by hypothetical Martian microbes may loom large in the public mind. Truly effective and reliable sterilization of the sample before return to Earth is so demanding as to delay the proposal a decade or more. Yet if sterile handling was necessary even for samples from the barren, atmosphereless Moon . . . ?

Science and Trans-science

The strength of science lies within the relatively narrow range of observable phenomena that are reproducible and recurrent. Once the scientist is driven out from that rather tightly controlled zone to deal with transitory, problematical, or extremely rare phenomena, no longer has he the full strength of the scientific method behind him. Ultimately he ends up using a mixture of intuition and crude "guesstimates" to form opinions. His opinions nevertheless may be the best around. But in this process he is particularly susceptible to incorporating his own value judgments into what is supposed to be an objective assessment of the problem.

We shall encounter trans-science throughout the subjects treated in this book. Environmental problems often present specialists with inadequate data to deal with very complicated environmental interactions, yet there is a real need for an "expert" opinion. Computer modeling of the interaction of population, world economy, and environmental change clearly carries the specialist into trans-science; the same computer models rarely can predict the past. More generally, much of social science necessarily involves trans-science, a source of criticism and misunderstanding by those whose reality is limited to "pure" physical science.

Trans-science is also concerned with the assessment of whether we are alone in the cosmos. Are there other intelligent societies elsewhere in the universe, very advanced compared to ours, with whom we may be able to communicate at some point in our future history? Here the fundamental questions are how often habitable planets form, and, on such planets, how often life develops and reaches the intelligent stage. Ultimately the scientist finds himself back in the land of trans-science.

Science and Miracles

Beyond the dimly lighted streets of trans-science is a region of phenomena I would term "miraculous." By miraculous I mean phenomena or events purported to have taken place which seem to defy the known "laws" of science. The occult has become big business lately. Even exorcism has been practiced with the tacit approval of the Roman Catholic Church. And there is increasing tolerance of the idea of religious miracles, especially those associated with healing. It is widely suggested that the state of health pertains to both physical reality and non-physical "psychical" reality.[31] It is asserted that truly organic healing has been accomplished through spiritual developments such as in some of the so-called miracles of Lourdes, as well as those reported to occur among some other religious groups.

It is very difficult to disprove such a possibility scientifically. The fact that some purported healings are later exposed as frauds, or, in some cases, of psychosomatic origin, does not necessarily mean that other purported cases are not significant. The sudden interest in the ancient practice of acupuncture can serve as a useful warning of how scientific skepticism in medicine sometimes reflects prejudice more than careful evaluation. When the phenomenon in question can really be observed reproducibly under controlled conditions, *then* the concepts of science change. Observations eventually overcome scientists' prejudices, as has been the case with meteorites, hypnosis, continental drift, germs, Troy, Atlantis, and Pleistocene Man, to cite just a few examples.

The great strength of science is that it is self-correcting, if enough "inexplicable" observations accumulate. Science is always a "best-for-the-time-being" explanation of observations. If the miraculous can be certified as physically real, then science expands, through theoretical insight, to incorporate the miraculous into the rest of observable physical reality. The miraculous is reduced to the ordinary.

How Science Changes

Science is that part of reason that can be verified experimentally. Accordingly, its boundaries change over time as new observations are acquired. Equally important, new world views arise, in which a vast amount of previously existing information becomes unified and more meaningful in the context of a new way of looking at it. For example, the basic facts necessary to deduce biological evolution had been available for some time before Darwin's voyage on the *Beagle*. But Darwin and Alfred Russel Wallace were among the first persons to look at the evidence in a different way, to recognize fully the significance of random genetic change combined with natural selection.[32]

The mature science of geology has been reborn in the last decade as the concept of plate tectonics and continental drift has revolutionized what had become a stalemated science. Suddenly a vast number of observations, in some cases known for almost a century, have been reunited in a new view of the Earth's history based upon the recognition that large portions of the Earth's crust have moved rigidly, relative to one another, throughout geologic time. Even forgotten and disregarded facts are being rediscovered. This new world view is still developing, leading to valuable new insights one after another within the subdisciplines of geology.

Much of human affairs swirls around science and technology in our stormy era. To navigate rationally and humanely we must appreciate the limits of science as well as its strengths. We must realize that there is no absolute way of viewing reality, but, instead, a multitude of world views inherited from many eras of man's cultural history.

SCIENCE AND MORALITY

Beyond the limits of science, beyond trans-science and miracles, is there a greater significance to the full physical universe which transcends the individual components sampled by science? Is there something moral, polarized, or spiritual encompassing the amoral material continuum perceived through our senses and described by science? Or is there nothing more to life than the hollow shell of mortality?

Astronomy, geology, archaeology, and biology showed that the basis of morality of established religions was mainly mythological—not historically accurate or physically credible. The allegories and pretty stories which provided an easily understood image of an exterior reality beyond the material were stripped away. Nothing has been substituted to provide a new source of authority for morality. Because the trappings have been shown to be created by men, not God, many presume the notion of a reality exterior to that perceived through our senses must likewise be a delusion. But that is beyond the realm of science to tell. If there is an aspect of reality beyond the material which can provide an independent basis for values, it cannot be obtained through the pathway of science. Nor can it be disproved through science.

Is There an Irrational Alternative?

The traditional conflict between idealism and materialism is as fresh and unresolved today as ever. Science can recognize no more than that rather narrow range of observable phenomena which qualify as reproducible and recurrent. Yet popular concepts of morality, of aesthetics, and of course of mysticism imply more than the material world of our senses. Most people (including scientists) *act* as if there is much more to reality than just the entire physical continuum which scientists try to understand. It is precisely from this disparity that the current crisis of spirit and intellectual ferment arises.

Recently there has been an irrational reaction in some quarters against science and technology. Scientists and engineers are perceived to maintain a comfortable alliance with the corporate and governmental establishment and thus obstruct what are deemed necessary social changes.[33] To others, technologists are culpable for the rape of the environment and the dehumanizing of modern city life.

But the answer does not lie in being irrational. It lies in understanding the limits of science and recognizing when it has been misused to address questions of value. The credibility of an exterior reality, of an absolute basis for morality or behavior, must involve more than can be learned from reproducible observations of nature alone. Man's spirit can be reunited with his body only in a reality that has room for both.

Scientists and Scientific Materialism

Among most fellow scientists I usually encounter humanistic values, but often without a clearly articulated basis. They are "for" the environment, personal and intellectual freedom, diversity of consciousness, and reflect compassion for others. Yet, like many in our society who have strong feelings about right and wrong, they do not have a well-worked-out theology or philosophy to explain the origins of such values. This seeming lack of intellectual analysis of the "why" is in some ways a surprising attribute of individuals who are so skillful in analyzing the "how." It may arise from a benign, but restricted and materialistic, view of reality appropriate for day-to-day scientific research.

Biologists sense the unity of all living things as well as the functional limitations of the brain perhaps more than those who work in other scientific disciplines. Robert Sinsheimer has written eloquently of these limitations:

> The very opening lines of Winnie-the-Pooh provide my theme. Here is Edward Bear, coming downstairs now, bump, bump, bump, on the back of his head, behind Christopher Robin. It is, as far as he knows, the only way of coming downstairs, but sometimes he feels that there really is another way, if only he could stop bumping for a moment and think of it.
>
> Now Edward Bear or Winnie-the-Pooh as he was known to his friends was of course a bear of very little brain. But nonetheless I often think that these opening lines constitute a splendid parable of man and his whole scientific enterprise —that we perforce go bump, bump, bump along the paths of scientific discovery when had we but the acumen, the brain power, we could immediately deduce from the known facts the one right and inherently logical solution.
>
> And yet of course we don't have the acumen and we can't immediately deduce the right solution because, like Pooh, our brains too are really very limited compared to the complexity about us and the frequent immediacy of our tasks. And in simple fact what else can we sensibly expect when we are apparently the first creature with any significant capacity for abstract thought? Indeed, even that capacity developed primarily to cope with stronger predators or climatic shifts, not to probe the nature of matter or the molecular basis of heredity or the space-time parameters of the universe.[34]

Apparently the impression that biologist Sinsheimer has of the limitations of the brain is sufficient for him to question the existence of a nonphysical reality. I asked him, "Is there a basis for human values other than inherited, cultural, or genetic influences?"

> It's not really clear to me that there is. One can ask that a set of values be consistent in the sense that it lead to a social system in which that same set of values is preserved. But

clearly there must be more than one set of values of that type. Many people have tried to derive value systems out of nature, out of evolution, etc. I have never been very impressed by these other than as indications of the cultural or innate biases of the individuals themselves.

Sociologist Nisbet once also assumed a like view of the origin of man's values but has grown less confident of that opinion in the intervening years:

> I'm slowly developing the belief that there are recesses of reality that the scientific logical experimental view takes us into a little way, but not all the way. I am convinced there is an Evil and a Good, but I'm stuck with that. Twenty years ago I would have shrugged and said, "No, they are just different manifestations of social experience."

Among some modern biologists, social Darwinism still survives today in more sophisticated form. Biologist James Bonner (as we shall see in Chapter V) asserts that proposals for genetic engineering to "improve" man do not even represent a moral issue. Another well-known biologist, Roger Sperry, asserts that science can become "a source and arbiter of values and belief systems at the highest level," and "affords the most direct avenue to an intimate understanding with the forces that move the universe and created man."[35]

Structuralism—A Basis for Morality?

Biologist and philosopher Gunther Stent feels that the new concept of "structuralism" affords a resolution to the conflict between materialism and idealism. To him, evidently, the conflict is an illusion arising from how the brain receives information about the outside world. He implies that the *why* of value ultimately can be understood in terms of *how* the brain works:

It is only in the past 20 years or so, more or less contemporaneously with the growth of molecular biology, that a resolution of the age-old epistemological conflict of materialism v. idealism was found in the form of what has come to be known as structuralism. Structuralism emerged simultaneously, independently and in different guises in several diverse fields of study, for example in psychology, linguistics, anthropology and biology.

Both materialism and idealism take it for granted that all the information gathered by our senses actually reaches our mind; materialism envisions that thanks to this information reality is mirrored in the mind, whereas idealism envisions that thanks to this information reality is constructed by the mind. Structuralism, on the other hand, has provided the insight that knowledge about the world enters the mind not as raw data but in already highly abstracted form, namely as structures. In the preconscious process of converting the primary data of our experience step by step into structures, information is necessarily lost, because the creation of structures, or the recognition of patterns, is nothing else than the selective destruction of information. Thus since the mind does not gain access to the full set of data about the world, it can neither mirror nor construct reality. Instead, for the mind reality is a set of structural transforms of primary data taken from the world. This transformation process is hierarchical, in that "stronger" structures are formed from "weaker" structures through selective destruction of information. Any set of primary data becomes meaningful only after a series of such operations has so transformed it that it has become congruent with a stronger structure pre-existing in the mind.[36]

An example of a brain process that has especially interested me involves how the brain "sees." There must be an enormous amount of preconditioning of visual sensory data prior to delivery to the cognitive portions of the brain. Consider the information rate involved in visual perception. An ordinary television picture displays data rapidly enough to require a communication band width of about 3 megahertz (3×10^6 cycles per second). Yet the individual neuron paths within the brain transmit information at a very slow rate, about 100 hertz. There is nothing resembling a television coaxial cable within the brain, not even a "wire" capable of conveying faithfully an ordinary telephone conversation. Somehow hundreds of thousands of neurons in parallel transmit small amounts of transformed or coded information from the retina to the visual cortex.[37] There the coded information from both eyes evidently is reconstructed and the cognitive function of "seeing" begins. Still more processing follows because representations of visual images are somehow compared with remembered patterns so that identification of visual "objects" and other thought processes can take place.

Our "minds" are, indeed, isolated from direct sensory information by several stages of coding and processing. And surely the nature of those biological structures must have a great deal to do with how we perceive and describe reality.

I share Stent's optimism that apparently diverse artistic and scientific perceptions of physical reality eventually may be understood to involve similar structures and preprocessing of sensory data. And I find useful, although still primitive, his suggestion that the paradigm phenomena (world view) in scientific discovery really correspond to the development of a new "strong" structure in the cognitive process, thereby permitting old data to be viewed in a new light.

However, I do not think he really has resolved the materialism versus idealism conflict. Understanding better how we perceive still fails to define better what is good or bad, right or wrong, unless one already has accepted the limitations of scientific materialism. Scientific materialism by any other name still remains an incomplete description of reality.

So what do I believe? Am I content with the limitations of scientific materialism or do I accept a greater reality?

My view is that the consciousness and understanding of present-day man are minuscule compared to the total dimensions of reality (to, if you will, God's mind, in which all of reality is understood). We are to that cosmic understanding as an ant is to us. And surely the ant cannot imagine love, charity, compassion, beauty, or relativity. Thus I am not at all surprised that we have difficulty in reconciling how we feel about things with what we "know" about them.

We are such a primitive conscious creature—the first of this planet to contemplate itself and its role in the world. It must be considered the height of arrogance to suppose that we are complete in this process. That we encounter paradox is to be expected in view of our primitive understanding of reality. Paradox, like obscenity, is in the mind of the beholder, and, I might add, is a measure of one's ignorance.

Thus I consider scientific materialism to be a narrow description of reality. There must be many dimensions of reality outside that achievable through the techniques of present or even foreseeable science. And it is those dimensions which sometimes can be perceived intuitively, if imperfectly, in the same way the scientist can form an opinion of trans-science intuitively. It is in that more encompassing reality that the polarity of value is recognized, if only dimly and occasionally. We must recognize our cognitive limitations to understand our potential, to withstand the paradoxes of the present which would lead us down the pathway to nihilism.

Most importantly to future values, the great mass of present humanity believes in a definite right and wrong as pertaining to human situations—witness the appeals and slogans of politics in any country as an example. In most countries there is also, I think, a widely accepted, if sometimes unarticulated, view of a broader reality than the material one, although this view has certainly been modified by the widespread development of Marxism. The present amalgam of man includes a moral heritage, a broad spectrum of views concerning immaterial reality and the basis of right and wrong. That heritage is being rapidly modified under the crushing pressures of our times. Yet morality of some kind must exist for humans to relate to one another. What will be the basis of morality for our descendants?

Man's concept of himself is a world view, albeit a much broader and more important world view than those of science. The older world view of the Western world, God watching man's actions and setting standards for him, has been gradually breaking down for the last several centuries—especially as the scientific assaults on religious mythology have grown sharper. Thus the plight of modern man might almost be posed as "The Case of the Missing World View." We are all desperately in need of a new world view, consistent with the facts of science but much broader and more encompassing. The new world view must provide reasonable guides to how men should behave toward one another. We must know how to rise above animals and act like gods.

I assert the primary intellectual event of the next several hundred years will be the development of this new world view. The suffering and seemingly purposeless disorder and destruction which are the hallmarks of the twentieth century (and perhaps much of the twenty-first as well) will sharpen men's views of themselves and their world. It will create part of the basis of what must truly be a new theology whose effects may be even more enduring than those of previous great religions.

III

RUNAWAY WORLD

*

The murderer was a quiet boy who sat on the front seat and regarded me with pale blue eyes; the evangelist, easily the most popular boy in the school, had the lead in the junior play; the pugilist lounged by the window and let loose at intervals a raucous laugh that startled even the geraniums; the thief was a gay-hearted Lothario with a song on his lips; and the imbecile a soft-eyed little animal seeking the shadows.

The murderer awaits death in the state penitentiary; the evangelist has lain a year now in the village churchyard; the pugilist lost an eye in a brawl in Hong Kong; the thief, by standing on tiptoe, can see the windows of my room from the county jail; and the once gentle-eyed moron beats his head against a padded wall in the state asylum.

All of these pupils once sat in my room, sat and looked at me gravely across worn brown desks. I must have been a great help to these pupils—I taught them the rhyming scheme of the Elizabethan sonnet and how to diagram a complete sentence.

ANONYMOUS[1]

T HERE ARE FEW ADULTS who have not witnessed in our own lifetimes increasing pollution and crowding of the Earth. There is widespread (and scientifically credible) anxiety that somehow environmental degradation cannot long continue unchecked or a variety of disasters will befall us.

Recently American faith in increasing prosperity has wavered, even as much of the world struggles to avoid famine. And the blasts and shots of armies and terrorists make up the percussion section in the dissonant symphony of contemporary life. Doomsday literature has become so common we tend to tune it out.

Even looking just a few years ahead, I find deeply disturbing conflicts among what I would like to consider primary values: humanitarian regard for human life, democracy, and the preservation of nature.

As the traumatic closing years of the twentieth century unfold, there are varied reactions to environmental degradation and the imminent return of the four horsemen of our Apocalypse: dismay, helplessness, indifference, or compulsive anxiety.

But if we are to perceive even the faint outlines of future possibilities, we must separate the compulsion to do *something* now from a dispassionate attempt to understand the present. We must accept the possibility of real disaster if we are to develop enough insight and strength to prevent it.

Let us view a snapshot of our troubled planet as would an alien, and then consider what he would forecast *assuming present trends continue unchanged.* Such a future would be most undesirable from all points of view and, I hope, unlikely. Nevertheless, it forms the inevitable basis from which to consider other possible futures in later chapters.

THE ARITHMETIC OF FAMINE

The population of the world is now four billion and *doubling* every thirty-five years or faster.[2] Unless checked, it will rapidly reach eight billion, sixteen billion, even thirty-two billion or more until literally there will not be enough space in the world for mankind. Aside from the shortage of food, who could look forward to living in a world saturated by the human species? Such a world would be hopelessly overcrowded; individual privacy and rights would be too restricted for life to be tolerable for human beings as they are now constituted.

The Crunch

Thus we are now entering into a crisis unique in the history of the world, which will profoundly affect nearly everyone reading these words. It is the people of this generation and the next two who will be the principal actors in this drama, the world of our children as well as ourselves. It is not a vague prospect for the future; it has started. I term this critical time period into which we are now entering "the Crunch." After the Crunch must come a leveling off of population and what must be a profoundly different era in world history, which I term "the Afterward."

Explosive population growth has become so critical to the world's future that a number of top-flight physical scientists have left their original disciplines to commit their talents to understanding its causes and effects. Roger Revelle was one of the leading oceanographers in the world when he left the Scripps Institution of Oceanography to establish a department of demography and population studies at Harvard. Harrison Brown of Caltech worked on the development of the atom bomb in World War II, then migrated into geochemistry in the postwar years. However, the world-wide population increase and resultant hunger and deprivation so obsessed him that he left geochemistry to become fully concerned with problems of population and resources.

Nobel prize-winning nuclear physicist Glenn Seaborg,

formerly Chairman of the Atomic Energy Commission and past president of the American Association for the Advancement of Science, has joined them in efforts to focus American financial and technical help for the developing nations.

Harrison Brown, biologist James Bonner, and world health authority John Weir carried out a study in 1957 entitled *The Next Hundred Years*,[3] in which they attempted to forecast the growth of population as well as of food and energy supplies. Ten years later, in 1967, they convened a conference entitled "The Next Ninety Years."[4] At that point, they and other specialists reviewed the forecasts of ten years before and found the 1957 estimates of population growth too conservative (as had been the case with the previous studies). Most importantly, the *rate of growth* of population had increased much more rapidly than expected; world population growth is accelerating rather than decelerating. Moreover, they found agricultural production had increased far less rapidly than had been hoped ten years earlier, with the result "that hunger is far more widespread in the world today than it was ten years ago." In addition, the developed nations were getting richer and industrialized more rapidly than forecast ten years prior, but economic growth in the so-called developing nations was found to be taking place far more slowly than anticipated. Brown commented, "It is absolutely clear the gap between the rich nations and the poorer ones is increasing rapidly."

United Nations statistics of the early 1970's continue the same story: the rich had been getting richer, the poor merely more numerous.[5] The tenor of *The Next Ninety Years* is more pessimistic and despairing than the attitude reflected in *The Next Hundred Years*, written a decade earlier.

The Urban Implosion

However, global population curves do not tell the whole story and can obscure a very important aspect of the population problem. The population increase is much, much larger within the underdeveloped countries than it is in the developed, in part as a result of the advent of antibiotics after World War II. Birth rates in the developed countries are dropping even more rapidly than had been predicted, just as in the developing countries they have grown more rapidly than predicted. Even so, the developed countries will become still more crowded because of increasing longevity and the large number of young women in the current population. But there is the expectation of an eventual stable balance with livable if not ideal conditions, around 400 million persons in the United States, for example.[6]

By comparison, the population of Mexico has increased from twenty million in 1940 to sixty million now; a population of over seventy million is forecast by the end of this decade. If present rates somehow persisted for the next hundred years, Mexico would contain well over *one billion persons*—more than the combined populations of the U.S. and U.S.S.R. predicted for that time. But Mexico will never be able to support a billion people. Thus the birth rate must drop dramatically or the death rate will skyrocket.

The rapid growth of population in the developing countries carries grim implications. Rural areas generally continue to support approximately as many people as always. The inexorable migration of the excess population of the developing nations is from rural areas to the cities—cities that are growing at an incredibly rapid rate without adequate economic or social bases. World-wide population explosion carries with it a fierce urban implosion. Urban areas of the developing nations perhaps are the greatest tragedy of the overall population growth in the world, with the least hope of solution of their problems. The growth of slum-ridden sprawls in Latin America, Asia, and Africa leads to political instability as well as to economic tragedy that now seems almost beyond the reach of humane policies.

Is Famine Inevitable?

Successive stages of the arms race have preoccupied American national consciousness since the end of World War II. But most of the peoples of the world have been caught up in a less glamorous but equally deadly race—population growth versus increase of food supplies. For nearly thirty years major famine has been avoided only through remarkable increases in agricultural productivity.

But the desperate race to avoid famine is looking less hopeful. We are entering a new era of global food shortages; per capita food production in the underdeveloped countries is starting to drop after small but consistent increases in the fifties and sixties.[7] The surplus food of the United States is not adequate to support the world's poor, even if we place charity high on our national priorities; the *annual* increase of world population alone is seventy million—equal to one-third of the total U.S. population. There is even some evidence of a small but devastating climatic shift, bringing catastrophic drought to sub-Saharan Africa—and perhaps elsewhere, in time.

Is global famine inevitable? Will the early mortality and privation of Malthus, rather than reason and compassion, once again regulate our numbers? Are we, after all, indentured serfs of the Animal Kingdom, the hopes of Science and Christ nothing more than passing heresies?

The humanitarian response to this awful challenge logically has focused on (generally unsuccessful) efforts to reduce birth rates and (generally successful) efforts to increase food supplies. Massive U.S. foreign-aid efforts following World War II, totaling $100 billion and reflecting the genuinely altruistic motives of its citizens, may merely have postponed the Apocalypse a generation or two.

The "Green Revolution" has raised the hopes of Mexico, Southeast Asia, and India especially. High yields of basic grains have been achieved through use of specially developed hybrid seeds and by extensive use of fertilizers, pesticides, transportation, and irrigation. However, diverse natural strains of grain, though less productive, provide much greater intrinsic resistance to disease. Thus the vulnerability of new "wonder wheat" and "super-rice" to new plant epidemics is greatly increased. (Even in the United States 15 percent of the 1972 corn crop was lost to a new variety of blight.)[8]

And the coupling of high grain productivity with increased consumption of energy and petroleum-based products is of dubious long-term efficacy in greatly increasing world-wide food production. Indeed, India's 1974 food crop was endangered by a shortage of petroleum-based fertilizer.[9] The shortage was aggravated by increased U.S. domestic usage in response to record world food prices. Thus the "Green Revolution" unintentionally has placed India in direct competition with industrialized nations for basic raw materials now necessary for food production. Ironically, large-scale integrated farming operations devalue India's greatest natural resource—peasants.

Agricultural Hopes for the Tropics and Oceans

Other agricultural hopes of the fifties and sixties are fading also. While agricultural production from tropical areas can be increased, it is often a temporary increase. Tropical abundance of light, heat, and fresh water can deceive agricultural intuition developed in temperate zones. The limit to growth in the tropics is usually the paucity of minerals in the soil. Indeed, tropical ecosystems have developed remarkable mechanisms to conserve dissolved minerals which otherwise are rapidly leached from the heavily weathered soil.[10] The "slash and burn" practice yields only one or two crops before depletion of the soil necessitates clearing of new mature forest.

Actually, even highly productive temperate areas must ultimately replace the mineral content of their crops. An average acre yield of alfalfa hay (four tons), for example, removes as much potassium as is produced by the natural weathering of two tons of original granite. Ultimately, inorganic enrichment must become as necessary as more conventional organic fertilizers if high yields are to be sustained. In the tropics the mineral limitation is encountered far more quickly since natural tropical weathering removes key inorganic constituents of the soil extremely rapidly.

Hence the tropics intrinsically cannot support as high a population density as temperate zones. A further difficulty is continued emphasis on "cash crops" (like coffee) rather than on production of food supplies for local consumption. This practice often has been retained by local entrepreneurs who displaced the European colonialists, thus aggravating both the tendency toward unequal distribution of domestic incomes and increased dependence on imported food.[11]

The once limitless promise of the oceans also seems to have been nearly fully exploited. Indeed, overfishing[12] and pollution may yet reduce total oceanic protein yield.

The frontier era is over for planet Earth. There simply are not vast areas of potentially bountiful land (or sea) awaiting the magic of man's touch to become new cornucopias.

The Optimistic View

However, there are still optimists. They generally view the food-supply problem in market terms: supply will continue to rise to balance demand. Indeed, the prolonged period of rapid and sustained increase in world food production can be cited as evidence of just this phenomenon. And obviously the ultimate limits to cultivation of major food-producing countries have not actually been reached.

It is true that food shortages still may be alleviated by increased world food production—but at greatly increased prices. Thus the underdeveloped countries, especially those impoverished in oil or other raw materials which are also experiencing rapidly inflating prices, can only feed their populations with greater and greater balance-of-payment loss—precisely the reverse of the circumstances required for local economic development. But, for still obscure reasons, voluntary slowing of birth rates seems to occur only in conjunction with general economic growth and increase in personal income.

Thus the only humane solution to the population explosion that humanitarians like Revelle, Brown, and Seaborg can foresee[13] requires greatly increased technical and financial aid to underdeveloped countries from the developed countries. Brown has consistently recommended that about one percent of the gross national product of the developed nations be donated annually (along with substantial technical and managerial assistance). For the United States this would mean about ten billion (1972) dollars annually, which may be compared with the less than two billion involved in the current quite unpopular foreign-aid program.

Like so many other commodities in our current life, charity has been greatly devalued. Successful application of the Brown-Revelle-Seaborg approach to humane limitation of world population through world economic development would have been much less costly a decade ago than now. Today's price may be beyond even our capacity to pay, if not to give.

China and the Future

But where does China and its one quarter of all mankind fit in the dichotomy of rich and poor, of advanced and underdeveloped countries? Although the average standard of living is low, recent reports indicate a high degree of local organization with evident success in public health, for example. Furthermore, drastic measures, including massive invasions of family privacy and privilege, are reportedly being undertaken to slow population growth.[14] New slogans like "One child is too few, two children are just right, but three are a major error" are replacing early dogma, like that of Chairman Mao in 1957:

> I hope that these men [officials who wanted to check population expansion] will open their eyes to reality—truly recognize that our nation's 600 millions are both an objective reality and our greatest single resource, China's capital. The large number of our people is a very good thing, and one must absolutely not object to population growth.

With little aid from either the United States or Russia, China has developed the technological elements of modern weaponry—nuclear weapons and rocket-delivery systems, jet fighters and the beginnings of a navy. And China must contain large reserves of oil and other minerals which could be profitably extracted if modern (especially U.S.) technology and organizations were utilized. In terms of present consumption as compared to ultimate resources, China may be a very rich country indeed.

We all have an interest in China's success or failure. If she fails, then a billion more persons will be caught in the terrible arithmetic of famine. If she succeeds, it will be by establishing a viable alternative to the governing systems of Russia and the West. That, in turn, requires the development of a permanent means of ruling once the absolute authority of Mao has been terminated by his death. Diversity among the ways great nations rule themselves may be the best hope for diversity in all aspects of life.

Cultural and Political Resistance

This policy of restricting population growth in order to protect per capita consumption is not shared by all governments. The President of Senegal, in February, 1974, said that the vast continent of Africa is populated by only 350 million persons, but that it has a capacity to sustain a billion. In that case, however, Senegal itself would have to do considerably better in food production than it did in 1973, when its many deaths from famine necessitated aid from the United States and other countries.

The same point of view was expressed by the Algerian Minister of Information and Culture, Ahmed Taleb, who stated: "Africa is a semipopulated continent. Its territorial extension is several times that of Europe and we have scarcely a third of the population of that continent."

Olof Palme, Prime Minister of Sweden, urged against "freezing the growth" of the Third World, stating that overpopulation is chiefly a problem of the United States, Germany, England, etc., but not, for example, of the majority of the African countries.

China, hypocritically, has exploited Third World fears that the emphasis on population control in underdeveloped countries could be a means of maintaining present relative levels for the "satisfied" countries and thereby freezing not only the population ratio but unjust relations between the nations.

The Argentine government in January, 1974, declared as its official policy an *increase* in population partly on the basis that "to govern is to populate." The actual reason may be fear of domination by Brazil's reckless economic and demographic growth. The Argentine government will inaugurate a new campaign to promote larger families in addition to other measures. Argentina also voted in the United Nations against the resolution to recommend family planning as a means to help relieve the problems of food shortage and underemployment.

Daily the tension grows, both in word and action. The charge is made that the developed nations are the cause of the misery existing among wide sectors of the underdeveloped countries. Little mention is made of the enormous contrast between wealth and poverty within those countries or the disproportionately small contribution by the rich through taxes for the support of the poor, especially in Latin America. Accusations made recently before the United Nations include: "The vast world of underdeveloped countries has paid too high a price for the prosperity of a few nations. . . . There is no charity in their aid—only self-interest." As in so much political rhetoric, both truth and appeals to hatred are intertwined. An almost suicidal paranoia seems to underlie the charge that the suggested coordination of population growth with food supply (especially in countries that even now suffer from hunger and malnutrition) is a smoke screen. The real purpose is inferred to be limitation of the economic growth and political power of the Third World. Similarly, the charge has been made that antipollution practices have been recommended to the underdeveloped nations in order to frustrate their industrialization.

But the saddest part of this Third World nightmare results from the failure of the Roman Catholic Church to contribute to the essential evolution of traditional attitudes toward birth control. The dominant hierarchy (mainly celibate European men) remains unable to this day to acknowledge the need for positive birth control measures. Indeed, Pope Paul recently has reiterated his opposition to any form of abortion—even when knowledge exists of genetic damage to the fetus, or when abortion is necessary to save the mother's life. (Ironically, abortion most often arises in those circumstances where the couple involved lack the knowledge or approval to apply birth control techniques.) As a result, even the heroic leadership—and sometimes martyrdom—of young Catholic priests in the cause of social progress throughout Latin America and parts of Africa may, in the long run, be of less significance to billions yet unborn than the inescapable reality of starvation and deprivation they will probably face. The anger and anguish of those billions may constitute the death rattle of the Roman Catholic Church.

The dominant social fact of the twentieth and twenty-first centuries is clearly the population explosion. Famine is alive and well in Africa[15] and is expected soon on every continent. The very essence of humanitarian value is being challenged. If industrialized nations become inured to widespread starvation elsewhere, psychological and philosophical changes surely will result; the unity of man will become a caricature rather than a vision. Faith was destroyed in the nineteenth century and Hope is failing in the twentieth. Will Charity become obsolete in the twenty-first?

ENERGY, ECONOMICS, AND THE ENVIRONMENT

The world of the rich is threatened also. Not only is population exploding, but average consumption per person is increasing at a high rate. The extraction and distribution of natural resources and energy supplies are increasing phenomenally, with doubling times as short as ten years to support the steady increase of consumption in the developed countries since the end of World War II. Consumption in many underdeveloped countries has also increased, although at a much slower rate. Roger Revelle has remarked that each American walks with a heavy step. He consumes 130 times as much as the average Indian (energy, basic food, and raw materials).

The Era of Global Shortages

Clearly this extraordinary increase of consumption cannot continue indefinitely. The Earth is not infinitely rich in materials that can easily be extracted nor in food that can be grown. During the last several years, even in the United States, significant shortages of protein and energy have begun to emerge. A new era of economics for the entire world, an Era of Global Shortages, is upon us— ready or not. A new era of politics must be expected as well.

The first energy shortage of crisis proportions in peacetime shook the Western world to its foundations in 1973.

The price of oil suddenly increased fourfold, equivalent to a yearly jump in cost of $75 billion—more than all the gold and currency reserves in all the treasuries of the world. And there seemed no alternative to accepting it. The Western world had rapidly increased petroleum consumption for two decades; new coal, natural gas, and nuclear power technologies had been ignored or delayed because they were deemed too costly as energy alternatives to petroleum.

Global shortages had been anticipated.[16] But they arrived somewhat earlier than anticipated, the result of underestimation of population and consumption growth and overestimation of new resource development. Thus the tragedy had been announced in the program notes, but we were surprised to encounter it in the second act instead of the third.

The year 1973 shocked America, Japan, and Western Europe into the realization that perpetual increase in their affluence can no longer be taken for granted. The sudden change from a buyers' to a sellers' market in the world's natural resources is making obsolete the twofold characterization of nations as "rich/poor," "advanced/ emerging," or the more tactful terms, "developed" versus "underdeveloped," "developing," or "less developed." Per capita income has long been an inadequate descriptor of "poor" nations like Mexico and Brazil, where the gap between rich and poor is much greater than in a "rich" country like the United States.

Less simplistic categorizations are beginning to emerge. An oil company president sees his world in a threefold categorization: (1) industrialized nations abruptly losing their cheap raw material imports; (2) emerging raw-material-rich nations swamped by riches and power; and (3) poor nations without abundant natural resources.[17] In mid-1973, Japan seemed close to achieving through industrialization and trade what its military aggression in World War II unsuccessfully sought—world economic leadership. Then the fourfold oil price increase later that year exposed the Japanese for what they really are—an extraordinarily energetic and organized people crowded onto vastly overpopulated, resource-poor islands. The same oil-price explosion that made Venezuela the most important country in South America also may have been a death warrant for millions yet unborn in Bolivia, Guatemala, and India.

The United States is rich in oil and probably richest in the world in coal and oil shale, with reserves equivalent to perhaps ten times the oil of the Middle East. But our lust for consumption (enhanced by the seductive sayings of Madison Avenue) has placed us now among the oil-importing nations. And our failure to focus our technological capability and capital resources on developing new coal and oil shale extraction methods means we must suffer severe economic dislocations for perhaps a decade or more. In the meantime, the Soviet Union should be relatively immune to the energy-price inflation. It has been their practice to keep domestic oil production and consumption closely balanced.

It is a bit ironic to read *The Next Ninety Years* now and consider what further changes may be necessary in the estimates made in 1967. The one ray of hope Harrison Brown held out for both the United States and the world was the prospect of the widespread use of cheap nuclear power. Even that hope has proven illusory for the coming decades. Just how effective the United States will be in meeting its energy needs remains to be seen, but it is quite unlikely that the energy produced will be cheaper than that previously obtainable. Thus even most of the developed/advanced/rich nations are down to the point of hoping for a miracle to avoid sharply increased energy costs and consequent leveling off (or reduction) of per capita consumption. The miracle in question would be a major discovery pertaining to nuclear fusion (or a related nuclear process), making a novel source of nuclear power feasible *and available* for large-scale production of electric power within a decade or so.

Will Technological Innovation Bring Back Abundance?

Is man's proclivity to use advanced technology as a substitute for social decision-making—for establishing priorities—finally running its course? Is there no hope for some new technological device or discovery which will relieve man from coming to terms with himself, his fellows, and his environment?

Whether new technological advances can—and will—continue to raise man's standard of living despite his explosive population growth is currently the topic of serious scholarly debate.

The Limits to Growth presented in 1972 the technological pessimists' view: explosive growth of global consumption very likely means world catastrophe within fifty years owing to both exhaustion of natural resources and pollution.[18] Technological optimists have responded.[19] The most cogent arguments are probably those of Starr and Rudman, who argue that technological growth is exponential and largely responsive to societal demands.[20] The limits to growth, in the optimists' view, are human expectations and resources, not natural resources. Technology can provide solutions to pollution and will do so when society gives it sufficient priority and removes institutional roadblocks. Thus the technological optimists' view is similar to the "economics" view in world agriculture.

It is difficult confidently to choose between the optimistic and pessimistic outcomes on an abstract basis—this is the domain of trans-science more than of science. It is clear that there are real limits to *rate of growth*. Nature may constitute a nearly infinite storehouse of potential sources of raw materials and energy, but the rate at which we can discover and exploit them is limited by both individual creativity and social organization. We are in the midst of a deadly serious race of rates: new means of extraction and exploitation of resources versus relentless population increase. The great imponderable is whether society—global society—will evolve rapidly enough to forestall the otherwise inevitable disaster. Will man outgrow disorganization, confusion, ignorance, indolence, national vanities and dreams of conquest, greed, the need to dominate others and feel superior? Will he leave behind these elements in today's human motivation, and yesterday's? They are present realities, but not necessarily part of the eventual future reality. Man has proved that he is capable of other motivation as well—courage, sacrifice, mutual aid, love—though these cannot in the present and the near future spare him the sufferings of the Crunch, which has already started.

It has always been true that the pursuit of individual self-interest was not necessarily in the best interest of the community of men (Adam Smith notwithstanding). It is only recently that the consequences of that paradox have become global. Thus we are in an unprecedented period of global interdependence.

A judicious blend of technological development and coordinated social change can avoid global disaster. But the computer models of neither the optimist nor the pessimist can confidently predict whether the requisite technological and social evolution will develop quickly enough. Since the present is unprecedented, the future cannot be predicted mechanistically. One can merely as-

sert one's intuition—social and technological intuition—
about the prospects.

Meanwhile—The Environmental Trauma Accelerates

By comparison, the environmental consequences of the
global consumption explosion are immediate and inescapable—rapidly spreading pollution, even to the very ends
of the Earth.[21] Indeed, visible pollution and environmental degradation generated grass-roots political reaction in
the United States during the sixties, uniting liberals and
conservatives, young and old, the White House and Congress.

By 1969 genuine progress in environmental protection
started to be codified in federal law, aided by President
Nixon's strong personal support. Truly significant accom-
plishments took place in the initial years of his Administration through the Environmental Protection Agency
and its three-man parent body, the Environmental Quality Council.

But in late 1973 the Arab oil embargo and accompanying escalation of world oil prices brought to a head the
inevitable conflict between energy, economics, and the
environment. In an incredible three months, virtually all
pending environmental restraints on the production,
transportation, and use of fossil fuels collapsed. The Alaskan oil pipeline was approved; deep-water ports for
supertankers and increased strip mining for coal were
authorized; auto-emission controls were postponed and
air-quality standards reduced to permit high-sulfur fuel
oil use; previously undeveloped wilderness areas of Utah
were leased for strip mining of oil shale; and coastal areas
offshore scenic Southern California beaches were readied
for lease.[22]

The last-named action surprised even the oil companies. My personal reaction was anger and dismay. I have witnessed since boyhood the uncontrolled conversion of Southern California from a natural paradise to urban sprawl, like the gradual change of a beautiful young woman to a degraded old one. But to debase the beaches and bay—to put in ugly drilling platforms (like those off Santa Barbara), with the inevitable oil spills, discharged drilling mud, and industrial flotsam and jetsam—that's too much for me to accept calmly. Is the free-running joy of my boyhood to be destroyed? Are our short-run fuel requirements that grave? Do the faceless officials involved in Washington really *feel* what their decision means to the special human pleasure represented by those beaches, or by the continued existence of the unspoiled wilderness of the Green River country of Utah, or of Alaska? (It is a tragic truth that one man's wilderness is another's wasteland.) Do their economic analyses balance those feelings, those aesthetic human values, against the economic value of using "our" oil instead of "theirs" for a decade or two?

Indeed, a hypothetical alien viewing our world from space might be puzzled as to why the United States, with such a high per capita consumption, is willing to degrade parts of what little natural heritage it has left to enhance that consumption marginally. We are really *consuming* our children's legacy of nature, not in the face of starvation, but in the midst of affluence. The hypothetical alien might wonder why the inhabitants of the richest country in the world sometimes *act* like the poorest peasants who are driven to eat their store of seeds reserved for next year's crop.

BURNING FUSES

Shortages in America and rapid increase in prices carry not only economic but political overtones. A principal characteristic of the American people has been a universal expectation of increased material benefits over time. That vision of the "American Dream" has been extended to a broader and broader section of the populace of this country, especially since the beginning of the New Deal in 1932.

Pressures for Renewed Imperialism

Yet it is not at all clear that this dream can be further realized; it certainly has not been so far in the 1970's. Real spendable income of Americans has been declining steadily in each recent year—as much as 4 percent in 1973[23]—and continues to. In addition to shortage-induced inflation, the increase in the average age of the population may mean reduced opportunities for advancement by the young. Reduction in personal freedom due to increased population places further limits on the American Dream. The American future is not likely to be a simple extrapolation of the American experience of the past.

Increasing economic pressures, and especially growing dependence upon foreign sources of energy and other resources, might tempt the United States into a new era of imperialism. The optimism and hope of "the war to end war," and "the war to make the world safe for democracy," have faded. The population of the United States has taken on a more realistic, perhaps more cynical, view of the world. The temptation to use military force, not in ideological conflict as was the tragic case in Vietnam, but rather for material benefit, may assert itself. If there are serious disruptions to the supply of copper from Chile, or oil from Venezuela or the Middle East, why not use the threat of military force, if not the actuality of it, to achieve economic goals? Indeed, Secretary of Defense Schlesinger, in late 1973, hinted at such a possibility by commenting that "Arab nations risk increasing U.S. public demand for force against them if they carry their oil embargo too far." An angry Arab denunciation followed immediately, rejecting the "diplomacy of the gun."[24] Although later improved relations were re-established between the United States and most Arab nations, those angry words and hard thoughts can hardly have been completely forgotten or the causes banished forever.

It can be argued that the United States no longer practices gunboat diplomacy because of our concern for relations with China and Russia, and, to a lesser extent, because of Communist and other revolutionary groups in the very countries we would threaten. I am inclined to emphasize also the traditional restraint which arose from the semialtruistic attitude of the American people following World War II. Regardless of the private viewpoints of political leaders, many Americans felt their country had a special responsibility to exercise international restraints to lead the world in humane endeavors and work toward peaceful means of solving international problems through the United Nations and otherwise. An example of this attitude was the support for Eisenhower's intervention in 1956 against the French and British to discourage them from carrying through gunboat diplomacy against Nasser's Egypt. Yet I wonder how strongly the United States would resist a European intervention in the Middle East now, say, to regain control of the oil-rich/people-poor Trucial States.

In the last two decades we have lost faith in our ability to lead the world in humane endeavors and to settle conflicts by peaceful means, especially through the United Nations. Thus renewed tendencies toward imperialism by the United States and by other advanced countries could surge in the coming decades. Such an outcome would carry with it the potential of armed conflict among the Big Powers. An era is at hand where there must be increased world governing by bilateral and multilateral arrangements among the major powers of the world, including economic matters, or the dangers of nuclear war will have to be faced as unrestrained rivalry driven by economic necessity takes place around the world.

The Armament Boom

The magnitude of the accumulated destructive power presently available in deliverable nuclear weapons is staggering. The equivalent of perhaps ten tons of TNT for every living person in the world patiently awaits Armageddon. Furthermore, as much as 10 percent of all human effort currently is devoted to the utilization, development, and fabrication of weapons and to dealing with the consequences.[25] An alien observing us from afar might wonder why we work so hard to prepare to kill each other—why Satan, not God, receives a tithe.

Of course, the SALT agreements and growing economic relations between the Soviet Union and United States can be regarded as indicative of a significant reduction in the chance of a cataclysmic nuclear World War III.

Yet the present tendency toward parity between the two superpowers carries with it curious and unsettling side effects. Both have become less able to manage the affairs of the world. While the Soviet Union and the United States acted out their symbiotic paranoia by amassing enormous amounts of refined weapons and delivery systems, Britain, France, and, more recently, China have accumulated smaller but still significant arsenals as their visible badges of Big Power status. It is no accident that the five permanent members of the Security

Council are also the first five nuclear powers of the world. Then India's detonation of a "small" nuclear explosive demonstrated the obsolescence of even the Security Council "Nuclear Club." The percussion of three atmospheric nuclear blasts within one day (India, China, France) ushered in a new era.

Proliferation of Nuclear Weapons

So far, the five permanent Security Council nations have shown restraint by not helping other nations to acquire nuclear weapons technology and therefore national nuclear arsenals. After long negotiations, the Soviet Union and United States, in June of 1968, together pushed through the United Nations the Non-Proliferation Treaty. As of the end of December, 1971, however, only about half the countries of the world had signed and ratified the treaty. Nations which have not signed include Brazil, Argentina, Cuba, India, Israel, Japan, North Korea, Pakistan, Saudi Arabia, South Africa, Spain, Tanzania, North Vietnam, and Zambia. Others which have signed but not yet ratified include Egypt, West Germany, Indonesia, South Korea, Turkey, Venezuela, and South Vietnam.

Virtually every region of current tension as well as many sites of traditional rivalries and hatreds are represented in these lists. Of course, there are many reasons for non-nuclear countries to avoid or to delay approval. In some cases, however, the stated or inferred policy is to keep open the option of acquiring nuclear weapons at some future time.

The Stockholm International Peace Research Institute has noted that of the fifty or so countries which have not signed and ratified the treaty, at least fifteen can be termed "near nuclear" countries,[26] including many in areas of severe tension. They may be expected to obtain the capability for production of nuclear weapons within the near or medium-range future, as India has done. Indeed, India, once the symbol (in Western eyes) of nonviolence, reportedly is now collaborating actively with Argentina to pioneer what may be the first South American nuclear power (and bomb) technology. South Africa not only is expected to have shortly the industrial capability for production of nuclear weapons but has the largest uranium reserves in the world.

Whereas Spain, for example, may not have much evident need for nuclear weapons, Australia (in the more distant future) may perceive circumstances for which it wishes an independent deterrent. Similarly, Japan, the third most advanced country economically in the world, is disproportionately weak militarily. An historic turning point must be near for the Japanese either to establish a lasting and mutually satisfactory partnership with China or to develop the first-rate nuclear deterrent required of a Big Power.

Following the October, 1973, Middle East War, Arab leaders discussed the need for an independent Arab nuclear capability.[27] Such aspirations cannot be ignored entirely, considering the enormous dollar resources available. There even have been rumors that France had been offered oil production from Libya in return for nuclear power plants—and nuclear weapons. And the United States is "evenhandedly" promising both Egypt and Israel to develop nuclear power plants. In countries with native competence in physics and technology, nuclear power technology must be regarded as a steppingstone to nuclear bomb technology.

The Soviet Union may have introduced nuclear-tipped surface-to-surface missiles into Egypt in conjunction with the October, 1973, Middle East War. If true, this was an unexpected and seemingly unwarranted escalation in the potential conflict.[28] Perhaps the Soviets are reconciled to local nuclear conflict within the next decade or two and thus exhibit less restraint concerning "local" nuclear confrontation. Whether détente could survive the use of nuclear weapons on a local scale is a frightful question.[29]

Beyond the possibilities represented by the near-nuclear powers, smaller countries such as Cuba, or even well-financed guerrilla groups, potentially could accumulate a few primitive but still extremely destructive weapons through illegal means. Ineffective security measures at some nuclear industrial facilities in the United States are a chronic problem.[30] Opportunity for illegal acquisition of fissionable components will become much more common as the world-wide use of nuclear reactors becomes more widespread. Fast liquid-metal breeder reactors are expected in the 1980's which will produce more plutonium than they use. If the continuing hostility and confrontation between the United States and the radical Cuban government were to continue for another decade, some unexpected series of events, perhaps triggered by a confrontation over the Guantánamo Naval Base, conceivably could lead to the threat (or even the reality) of a primitive nuclear bomb attack on Miami by a desperate Cuban government.

Tactical-Weapon Proliferation

The growing inability of the Soviet Union and the United States to control world affairs is apparent even in the area of tactical weapons. The October, 1973, war included full-scale application of first-line aircraft, antiaircraft missiles, and antitank missiles by both Arab and Israeli armies.[31] For the first time since World War II, the superpowers really could not have intervened on a tactical level without either using weapons of mass destruction or accepting high casualties themselves. By comparison, in past decades, both the United States and the Soviet Union have retained the latest aircraft and other tactical-weapon systems for their own use. Older weapons were distributed to their satellites and allies.

This is no longer the case in the Middle East. Furthermore, purchase arrangements between Saudi Arabia and France for large amounts of new first-line aircraft and other kinds of weapons in exchange for oil could portend further expansion of this situation.[32] Ultimately the United States and the Soviet Union conceivably may face an uncontrollable tactical military situation in the area.

Burning fuses connect both conventional and nuclear weapons to traditional hatreds and renewed competition for resources. Tensions run high among new nations, sometimes not separated by natural geographic or ethnic boundaries. While the prospect of global war and annihilation of the Earth may be declining at present, the prospect for overheated regional war may well be increasing to test anew planet Earth's capacity for world governing.

THE "THINGS TO COME" SCENARIO

What can prevent runaway destruction in the new era of global scarcity and famine—or head off runaway pollution before toxic environmental conditions are reached? Obviously an increased degree of world cooperation and responsibility is essential. But suppose the nationalistic rivalry which has been the tragic hallmark of this century continues unabated throughout the remainder of it? Suppose national antagonism continues to be a stronger force in world affairs than fear of global disaster?

H. G. Wells Revisited

A fictional world of this type was forecast by H. G. Wells in his 1932 novel entitled *The Shape of Things to Come.*[33] Rereading Wells' novel more than forty years after it was written brings to one's attention many things about which he was wrong. For example, he argued that the great depression of the thirties would not end for many decades and would itself cause the collapse of the industrialized nations of the world. He missed entirely the significance of the population boom and global pollution. He did not foresee the rapid progress toward the equality of women, of minorities, and of non-European countries. He forecast recurrent wars but did not contemplate the singular disaster of World War II. And he relied on a rather naïve "wings of the world" cabal to establish successfully a Modern World State after the main collapse. Thus he still managed to find a happy ending (after about A.D. 2100).

Nevertheless, some of his insights are of interest even forty years later. For example, the unpredictable character of nineteenth- and twentieth-century history impressed him, as indicated in this excerpt from a purported twenty-first-century history book:

Because of this belatedness of the social sciences, the progressive dislocation of the refined if socially limited and precarious civilization of the more advanced of the eighteenth and nineteenth century sovereign states went on without any effectual contemporary understanding of what was straining it to pieces. The Europeans and the Americans of the early twentieth century apprehended the social and political forces that ravaged their lives hardly more clearly than the citizens of the Roman Empire during its collapse. Plenty and the appearance of security happened, then debacle happened. There was no analysis of operating causes. For years even quite bold and advanced thinkers were chased by events. They did not grasp what was occurring at the time. They only realized what had really occurred long afterwards. And so they never foresaw. There was no foresight, and therefore still less could there be any understanding control.[34]

Wells pictured warring nationalistic states first accelerating the growth of technology, then overextending themselves by carrying out such great mutual destruction as to reduce global technological capability. That scenario is a plausible outcome of the present unless world-governing systems develop soon and effectively. It can be avoided only if tendencies toward global governing accelerate.

Wells—Too Optimistic?

Actually, Wells was a bit naïve. He was too optimistic! During the growth of industrial civilization, man has exploited progressively lower-and-lower-grade ores and more and more sophisticated energy sources. If heavily armed nuclear nation-states cause world-wide disruption to take place, technological civilization will crumble. Harrison Brown envisions under such conditions that "the poor and miserable will then inherit the Earth and live miserably ever after." Inasmuch as high-grade resources and energy supplies will have long since disappeared, technological civilization will be gone, "never to rise again."[35] High-grade steel might be salvaged from the rubble of modern cities, but the sophisticated and vulnerable oil and nuclear power industries would be inoperable. Technology would once again be limited by availability of local energy sources except that now the shallow deposits of high-grade coal that fueled the first Industrial Revolution would not be available to permit a renewal of the process.

To bring these pessimistic scenarios into harmony with our modern, ecologically-oriented attitudes, it is also necessary to include almost total pollution of the Earth. In "Things to Come," as I now see it, a few billion (or less) would be living in subsistence conditions, racked by disease, ignorance, and other accompaniments of poverty. The natural Earth as we know it will have been destroyed. Technological civilization will have collapsed, to be replaced by some more barbaric forms of life. There would be little prospect of any Renaissance to follow such Dark Ages.

Updating Wells' ideas in the perspective of the 1970's leads to a very bleak picture, a tragic ending to man's great promise. Personally, I have more hope for man. There are strong tendencies visible throughout the world toward the development of international governing systems. Yet "Things to Come" must be recognized as a possibility for the future, against which must be weighed the sacrifices required for new solutions to global problems. There is no present social or political force which alone will prevent this outcome. Present rates of economic and population change imply disaster if unchecked. We must insist on accelerating tendencies toward new kinds of governmental configurations. "Things to Come" is a totally unnecessary, undesirable, no-win outcome of the present.

IV

A FUTURE ELSEWHERE?

*

A Martian Mother's Warning

Don't play around with astronauts;
    Beware, my darling daughter!
How can you trust such awful creatures
    Who breathe in air and swallow water?

They spy on us with flying saucers
    (Incredible but true)
And just because they envy us
    Our delicious CO_2.

CHURCHILL MURRAY[1]

T HE, DISMAL FUTURE of the Earth projected from present trends has fueled the creative minds of science-fiction writers for many decades. They have contemplated the possibility of the human race proceeding outward from this planet to another habitable planet and re-establishing civilization there. The advent of the Space Age has enhanced such expectations, for the image of man going as far at least as to the Moon has now become commonplace. Travel to deep space is widely accepted as a part of future reality; dramatic works such as *2001: A Space Odyssey* present with convincing realism the means for human beings to explore distant realms.

Recently a high NASA official proffered his view of the future:

I firmly believe that among the billions of planets out there in other solar systems there must be a few which have life as we know it. . . . We will find that this is not the only place where people can live, and as we lose more of our freedoms here on earth, missions to these other solar systems will be a reality. . . . In another thousand years we may be faced with the necessity of leaving this planet.[2]

Thus it is not surprising that practical men often carry in their minds the dim prospect of human colonization of nearby planets or even those of a distant solar system. Among the more anxious, the possibility of planetary colonization sometimes looms up as an actual necessity for survival of the human race.[3]

For those who are most anxious about life here on Earth, bizarre UFO reports in the popular press suggesting visits from advanced extraterrestrial societies can become significant. Are aliens already traveling between habitable planets?

A great deal of information has been acquired in the last ten years about the nature of the most popular planets for colonization—Mars and Venus; we can assess the practicality on a more scientific basis than was possible previously. In addition, we now have some Space Age experience on which to estimate the time and effort necessary for the development of exotic new technology required for interstellar travel. Mankind can look forward to travel deep into space if desired. But should the human race mount a major effort to colonize other planets because the future here is so dismal? Could such action really blunt the frightful reality which seems to await us during the Crunch?

ENVIRONMENTAL REALITIES

In science fiction the most popular future home for mankind has been the planet Mars. Beginning with the vivid imagination of astronomer Percival Lowell, who imagined he saw a network of straight lines there, suggesting to him the handiwork of intelligence, both scientific and fictional minds have toyed with the habitability of Mars.[4] Originally it was imagined that Mars could be inhabited by human beings. More recently the expectation has been reduced generally to some very low form of life.

But the discovery by Mariner 9 in 1972 of so far unexplained earthlike features—great canyons, sinuous channels—has revived to some extent the idea of a habitable Mars. Indeed, astronomer Carl Sagan suggested recently the possibility of altering the climate of Mars by the introduction of dark, one-celled plant forms in the icecap areas to change the polar heat balance.[5] Two of his colleagues, Joseph A. Burns and Martin Harwit, have posed a more ambitious scheme, including the modification of the orbit of Mars to make the seasonal conditions more equitable for life.[6]

The reason for such imaginative attempts to modify the planetary environment is that the current environment is so very hostile to terrestrial life in any form, much less human life.[7] Pressure at the surface of Mars is less than one percent that at the surface of the Earth—similar to what would be encountered in an unpressurized aircraft at well over a hundred thousand feet elevation. We have altogether too much experience from terrestrial aviation accidents to know that the human body cannot survive even seconds in such low pressure. In addition, the atmosphere is not oxygen but carbon dioxide and is toxic for humans. Finally, the planet is very cold. It is farther from the Sun than the Earth and has no oceans or heat-absorbing atmosphere to provide warmth.

There is no place on Mars as comfortable and habitable as central Antarctica or the middle of the Greenland icecap! Mars is not a site for eventual human habitation unless some major planetary engineering is carried out which successfully changes its atmosphere and, in consequence, surface conditions to those more tolerable for human life. The time scale for this kind of activity is quite distant. Successful planetary engineering depends not only on the development of specialized technology but also on a thorough understanding of the present environmental conditions and interrelated processes.

In the case of Venus, the problem is heat, not cold. The surface temperature on Venus is nearly 900°F.(530°C.). All organic material would be dissociated and destroyed after only a brief exposure to these temperatures. In addition, the pressure is nearly a hundred times that at the surface of the Earth, comparable to what a human being would experience at a depth of about three thousand feet in the ocean. Venus is far less habitable than the ocean bottoms on Earth. Whereas on Mars the hypothetical human would both freeze and die by decompression instantly, on Venus he would boil and die from overpressurization in the same period of time. In both cases, he would be asphyxiated as well, since the atmosphere of Venus also is composed almost entirely of toxic carbon dioxide.

Planetary engineering in principle is also applicable to Venus. As early as 1961 Sagan proposed the possibility of implanting some resistant species of blue-green algae in the upper cloud layers gradually to convert the carbon dioxide into oxygen by photosynthesis, thereby producing both a less toxic atmosphere and a gradual reduction of surface temperature.[8]

But planetary engineering for Mars or Venus can be

considered only semiseriously. We know little about the environments and much less about the effects and side effects of introducing biological species into apparently sterile environments.

Neither planet is at all habitable in its present form, and the technical requirements to make them so could be achieved only in the remote future, if at all. Indeed, Burns and Harwit comment, "The proposal is, perhaps, a fantastic one to contemporary minds. However, it seems to us that the required technology will not be wanting if man is alive 10,000 years from now." Colonization of Mars or Venus does not constitute an avenue by which the human race can escape the awful choices and frightful destinies that may be ahead during the Crunch. It is at most an occupation to absorb excess terrestrial energy and imagination at some distant point Afterward.

But the imagination of man aspires beyond Mars and Venus. There has even been some discussion from time to time about the possibility of creating a colony on an asteroid, those small, lunar-like bodies that orbit between Mars and Jupiter. Even brief contemplation clearly indicates the special difficulties with such a concept. The surface of an asteroid is probably similar to that of the Moon except that the gravity is extremely low. In addition, because the orbit is not circular about the Sun, there is a strong seasonal effect. Hence the problem of establishing a viable human colony on an asteroid is considerably more difficult than that for the Moon, already known from the Apollo experience to require total isolation from the surface environment of the planet rather than adjustment to it.

Beyond the possibility of the asteroids, other objects within this solar system generally are not attractive even to science-fiction writers. Close to the Sun, the planet Mercury receives from six to ten times as much solar radiation as does the Moon and therefore would be an even more difficult place to colonize; it, too, is atmosphereless. Out beyond the asteroid belt and the orbit of Mars, the giant planets and satellites simply receive too little solar energy to support a human colony in the foreseeable future. Controlled nuclear fusion not only must have become a major terrestrial energy source, but that technology would have to become transportable through long space journeys before colonization there could even be contemplated.

If man is looking for habitable planets, why not in the environment of another star than our Sun? Indeed, many scientists reason that among all the stars in this galaxy similar to the Sun in general composition and energy radiation, it is plausible to assume that there are other earths as well. Even if one star in two hundred has habitable planets, there would be only about a hundred such planets in a sphere of one hundred light-years' radius.[9] Even traveling at the velocity of light, the travel times are beyond those of credible human lifetimes. Thus the practical journey to such a star would require not just technology that hasn't been invented but even physics that hasn't been discovered.[10] Hence the possibility of colonization outside our solar system belongs to the very distant future, after Afterward, if at all.

ECONOMIC AND SOCIAL REQUIREMENTS

There is a further objection to the concept of man's future being found elsewhere than on this troubled Earth. The provision of adequate technology, both to journey to another planet and to sustain human life there for any extended period of time, requires technological and economic support beyond that carried out by any nation on the Earth so far. That support, in turn, implies an economy of abundance to subsidize nonproductive ventures of such scale as well as a social organization conducive to massive technological efforts. These last two attributes are the very ones in jeopardy at present as the world's population strains available resources and governing systems to their very limits. It therefore seems to me especially unlikely that resources will be found to subsidize extraterrestrial colonization in the next hundred years, as distinguished from the simply venturesome space travel of limited numbers of highly trained astronauts and cosmonauts.

Another way of viewing the problem is that the environments of even the nearest planets are far more hostile than those of the most inhospitable areas on Earth—the icecaps of central Greenland or Antarctica, or the ocean bottoms. Hence one would expect colonization of the Moon or planets to take place only when extremely adverse, hostile environments on Earth are overpopulated. When central Greenland and Antarctica are overpopulated by self-sustaining colonies, then we might begin to wonder whether planetary colonization might follow.

There is no foreseeable economic benefit for Earth directly associated with materials that can be either fabricated on or returned from the planets. Hence any human activities there must be subsidized at very great cost. That, indeed, would be possible only if the people providing the subsidy, namely, those living on Earth, got some benefit from the existence of others living on other planets. In the case of Apollo flights to the Moon, this subsidy was based largely on a vicarious sense of adventure and national pride. Apollo was genuinely popular; the costs were willingly borne by the American people. Some governmental leaders also viewed Apollo as good Cold War competition, but I do not think such views were a major factor in Apollo's remarkably enduring domestic support.

Such political conditions may recur. There may be additional manned ventures into deep space driven by similar motives and appeal as Apollo; Soviet interest in manned space flight seemingly persists despite their difficulties in development of the requisite technology. On the other hand, Apollo may prove to have been the high-water mark in the competitive development of technology for technology's sake by the United States and the Soviet Union; Apollo may be looked upon a hundred years hence as a fantastic anomaly that took place in the midst of the Crunch.

WHY PLANETARY EXPLORATION?

There is no future for mankind elsewhere immediate enough to avoid the agonizing choices that lie ahead during the Crunch, or for some substantial period of time afterward. Not only are there formidable technical and environmental questions to be solved concerning the nearest planets, but the economic and social conditions on Earth will hardly be favorable for the support of colonization elsewhere during the crucial decades.

On the other hand, it by no means follows from this pessimistic appraisal of planetary colonization that the exploration of the planets is not a valuable activity. Indeed, the discovery and understanding of new worlds and the comparison of their histories with our own is a mind-expanding experience which ultimately modifies the consciousness of much of the human race. It is one of the few imaginative positive actions open to modern technological societies.

Planetary exploration provides food for man's spirit, not sustenance for his body. So much of what we do is necessarily negative, or, at best, neutral—war, pollution, industrialization. We, meaning the people of the industrialized countries, and especially the United States and the Soviet Union, have at this point the opportunity to contribute uniquely to the cumulative consciousness of mankind by exploring the planets and documenting those explorations in a manner amenable to understanding by the broad populace of the world. Such an activity to me is comparable to painting, music, and other forms of art.

Planetary exploration is a cultural activity America can carry out especially well, technologically and scientifically. This is the magic moment in man's history in which an extraordinary reaching outward is taking place. It would be sad if the industrialized United States became so absorbed in the necessities of the moment as to forgo activities aimed at future cultural benefits for which we are uniquely qualified. I think the rationalizations for support of planetary exploration and for supporting the arts are very similar. The only difference in the United States is that much of the money for supporting the arts comes from private and local subsidy as well as performance charges, whereas planetary exploration has fallen entirely under the aegis of the federal government subsidy. But if proper books were kept (which included both public and private funds and entertainment charges), and all cultural activities were evaluated jointly on a national basis, I think that the present balance between support for planetary exploration and that for other cultural endeavors would not be regarded as disproportionate. U.S. planetary missions over the last decade have averaged barely one dollar per American per year—less than a ticket for a single movie performance.

There are hidden benefits as well resulting from pursuit of planetary exploration. Rather than wonder why we should explore such inhospitable worlds, we might better ask, "Why are these worlds so uninhabitable?" Venus is the Earth's twin in size, mass, and bulk composition. In fact, planetologists generally agree that if Earth had been located 30 percent closer to the Sun (like Venus), it, too, would exhibit an enormously thick, hot, and poisonous atmosphere. Even though carbon dioxide constitutes only a trace of the Earth's present atmosphere, enormous quantities of that gas were evolved to the surface from the interior over our more than four billion years of planetary history. But our carbon dioxide was continually dissolved in the oceans and then precipitated as a solid compound, calcium carbonate. Immense quantities of calcium carbonate, thus formed, now reside as layers of limestone in all the continents.

But if Earth had been too hot for water to condense completely into oceans, an incredibly dense, hot atmosphere would exist here also and this planet would be uninhabitable, like Venus.

Thus the question remains: How much more sunlight can our planet absorb without the onset of unstable conditions? If temperatures were increased enough to create an exceptionally humid atmosphere world-wide, more radiant heat (infrared radiation) from the surface would be absorbed, in turn heating the atmosphere further—and so on. This circumstance, termed a "runaway greenhouse" effect, is one of the hypothetical consequences of intense world-wide air pollution. The release of excess carbon dioxide to the atmosphere as a consequence of rapid consumption of fossil fuels (as well as added absorption of radiant heat by particulate pollutants) already has been credited by some with small but measurable increases in local and global temperature. Just how sensitive is our global heat balance? Is there an eventual danger of a runaway greenhouse?

Of course such questions carry us into the domain of

trans-science. Precise estimates are not possible. Nevertheless, better understanding of a world that did succumb to the runaway greenhouse effect (Venus) may be helpful in sharpening our scientific intuition concerning the impact of global pollution on one that has not . . . yet.

Mars, on the other hand, may hold clues to the other climatic extreme—return to Ice Age conditions. A beautiful sequence of finely layered deposits discovered in the Martian polar regions by Mariner 9 may contain a record of past solar fluctuations highly pertinent to the origin of Earth's Ice Ages.

Furthermore, transparent pollutant particles at very high altitudes on Earth may be near the end of a geologically brief warm period. Certain kinds of global air pollution conceivably could hasten that change.

Surely, we live in too delicate a balance of natural and man-made phenomena not to be curious about our neighboring planets—and why they are uninhabitable.

There are, of course, immediately practical aspects of space activity like communication and weather satellites which can be justified on strictly economic grounds as well as unforeseen applications from the focused development of any new advanced technology—including those for space. Indeed, I feel we have reached the point now where manned Earth-orbital flights must also be justified in terms of at least plausible future benefits. The *exploration* of Earth orbit is over; the principal purpose in further Earth-orbital efforts, especially manned space flight, therefore must be utilitarian. But providing man's first look at his solar system neighbors remains one of the most exciting cultural endeavors for the next several decades. And it just might sharpen man's scientific intuition enough to help keep Earth from becoming like them.

V

DIMENSIONS OF THE FUTURE

*

"But if you know about God, why don't you tell them?" asked the Savage indignantly. "Why don't you give them these books about God?"

"For the same reason as we don't give them *Othello:* they're old; they're about God hundreds of years ago. Not about God now."

"But God doesn't change."

"Men do, though."

"What difference does that make?"

"All the difference in the world," said Mustapha Mond. . . .

Mustapha Mond shut the book and leaned back in his chair. "One of the numerous things in heaven and earth that these philosophers didn't dream about was this" (he waved his hand), "us, the modern world."

Brave New World[1]

WHAT WILL BE the world of the future?

Like the past and present, it can be described in terms of many parameters: politics, economics, wars . . . religion, ethics, mores and social patterns . . . or its undreamed-of inventions and architecture . . . or the language, music, art. How do I choose to describe the future?

The Descriptors—People, Governing Systems, Environments

Despite the almost infinite facets that will make up the world of tomorrow, of most interest to me are the people.

What will they be like—our children and our children's children—in the world of the future? How will our descendants live and think and feel a hundred years from now—or five hundred—or five thousand?

Will there still be the rich variety of consciousness and values that characterizes our turbulent present? Or will the relentless demands of the Crunch winnow man to a homogeneous automaton? Or will natural man become as extinct as natural corn and be replaced by an artificial, genetically domesticated form of life, literally created by man in his own image?

To be interested in people is to be interested also in how people relate to each other—because no man or woman can live by and for himself or herself alone. Similarly, no nation can live by and for itself alone; if it tries, history has shown how disastrous is the awakening. If the "Things to Come" scenario is not to become a reality, some mechanism to inhibit aggression by one state upon another must come about. A stable scheme to regulate the economics of the world and limit pollution, at least to prevent toxic levels, must evolve. Increased world governing is essential to a future worth waiting for. It is the second major descriptor of the future. What will be the source of authority for regional and world government? What will be the balance between force and authority?

Also, I am concerned about the nature of the environment in the world to come. If we are not to be a totally polluted planet, then what alternatives exist? What will be the nature of the physical and biological environment we shall pass on to our children, and they to theirs? Will there be any relics of the past left in the future, or will our planet be transformed into a completely artificial world?

The futures I can imagine are thus three-dimensional. They are constructed from and defined by: (1) kinds of people, (2) world governing systems, and (3) resulting global environment. "Things to Come" is an unhappy outcome of the present in which diverse people are unable to develop effective world governing. Global pollution is an inevitable consequence. Of more appeal are outcomes in which diverse people do establish effective means of world governing and also retain some natural environments.

But the full range of our three dimensions must include also the possibility of much greater uniformity in people and environments, even to the extreme of artificial people inhabiting an artificial planet.

Time scale, too, is important. In Chapter VI ("The Crunch") we shall consider three very different but entirely possible outcomes of the next hundred years. Chapter VII ("Afterward") deals with longer-term possibilities.

Here we review separately the future possibilities of each of our three chosen dimensions. First we shall consider the staggering potential for the replacement of the natural by the artificial—in environment, even in people. Then we shall examine the seemingly contradictory yet simultaneous current governmental trends toward homogenization and authoritarianism versus diversity and disorder. The eventual balance between these opposing trends in current society will influence markedly the kinds of people and the elements of world-governing systems of the future.

TOWARD AN ARTIFICIAL WORLD

What is the natural world? Man may soon forget. Ecologically, there are only a few areas left in the world that have escaped his obvious interference, none that do not contain at least telltale traces of his pollution.

Those who would try to create humane conditions for

the world's burgeoning population must necessarily make our planet more artificial than ever by a massive increase in urbanization as well as food supply. For example, urban planner Richard Meier proposes twin projects for underdeveloped nations.[2]

One is the development of the "nuplex" concept involving the use of a nuclear reactor for power, located near the coastline, where it can also produce desalinated sea water for irrigation and the necessary energy for farming and light industry.

Second, he advocates a totally different kind of city pattern in which human waste is recycled and used within urban areas which also include local crop growing, so that people can produce perhaps 70 percent of their food in the areas in which they live. Logical extension of this concept leads to the rapid growth of Tokyo-size cities all over the world, finally merging into huge metropolitan areas, especially along coastal plains. Thus he would provide a physical home and service area for additional billions.

The reverse face of the humanitarian coin seems to be virtually total conversion of existing natural areas into artificial ones.

The Extinction of Virgin Lands?

Of course, exploitation of virgin areas traditionally has been a means of easing political and economic pressures in previously settled areas; the brief history of the United States is a classic example. The current "economic miracle" of Brazil centers around the conversion of the Amazon Basin from a natural to a modified state, probably including unanticipated changes in climate.

A still hypothetical new approach to the difficulties

in the Middle East can further illustrate the fundamental environmental liability represented by humanitarian use of technology, planning, and capital resources to provide food and living space in an overpopulated world. A central political issue in the Middle East conflict has been the deep feeling of the Palestinian people that they have lost their home, physically and spiritually, as a result of the development of the state of Israel. The Israelis feel it is a question of the survival of their nation, perhaps their existence. Four times Arab armies have tried to restore the past. Four times bloodstained land has changed hands.

A lasting solution might develop if the presently uninhabitable Sinai Peninsula could be transformed into an arable region, perhaps by application of the nuplex concept. Suppose it were possible (with sufficient capital input from oil-rich Arab states?) to create fresh water and irrigate the Sinai Peninsula through the nuplex concept. A relatively self-sustaining area could develop, instead of the practically uninhabited wilderness in which only the Bedouin can live. A new land for at least some of the Palestinian people literally could spring from the desert, rivaling even the miracles of the Koran, Old Testament, and Torah. A long-term political solution for the Middle East, hypothetically at least, might arise through application of modern technology to a presently uninhabited area.

Ignoring the practical questions as to whether such technology is really economically feasible, and whether the peoples involved would cooperate to apply it, the possibility illustrates in contemporary terms man's ever-present pressure on the remaining natural areas. One more war and the United States could become an authoritarian state. And the best candidate for the cause of that war is, by common consent, the seemingly irreconcilable

differences between the Arabs and Israel. Perhaps the conversion of a natural area to an artificial one might defuse these modern Balkans awaiting their Sarajevo. Once again, man would sacrifice nature rather than come to terms with himself.

But whether or not the Sinai is radically modified, there are few virgin areas left anywhere. Eight thousand years of expansion into one frontier after another is nearly over —forever. Man *is* saturating the Earth.

The Extinction of the Oceans?

Each step toward making the Earth more bountiful brings additional environmental burden and likelihood of pollution. Materials are extracted from the Earth, they enter the water system and eventually arrive in the ocean; thus the very process of converting the land surface of the Earth fully to man's needs carries with it the implication of world-wide oceanic pollution. Until recently this possibility had seemed so remote that it had not even occurred to most people; the oceans of the world cover three-fourths of the surface; the continents are but islands in an enormous lake. The oceans have nurtured life for billions of years; furthermore, the salt and other minerals had seemed a cleansing and antiseptic solution as well as a nutrient for life. The oceans provide man with a major supply of food and are the chief source of protein for hundreds of millions of people. The ocean has been one of the resources to which man has looked to meet the needs of a much larger world population.

Yet Jacques Cousteau, long identified as a great popularizer of the beauty of the ocean and of its living entities and as a defender of the ocean against pollution, seems to have accepted the prospect of a totally polluted ocean

arising relatively soon along with global ecological catastrophe.[3]

Assuredly the changes in the character of the ocean and the demise of its natural state are going on at a frightening pace. If man does successfully convert the entire land surface of this planet to his uses, he will be faced with re-engineering the oceans soon afterward, merely to keep pollution below toxic levels. The concept of an artificial planet carries with it the necessity of a closed system— complete recycling—in which no one portion, especially oceans, can be ignored because it will inevitably end up as a sink for wastes and thus negatively influence other environments.

Retention of Some Natural Environments?

What other alternatives may exist besides that of either the totally polluted world or the artificial planet?

It is already too late for us to talk about a completely natural world. However, some areas still remain, with little visible evidence of man's modification, due either to their inaccessibility or to their uninhabitable character. Or, as in the case of the National Park system, they are aesthetically pleasing and healthful areas whose use is maintained in a way consistent with retaining most of their natural attributes.

Thus future environments can be totally polluted, completely artificial, or mainly artificial with selected natural areas, depending upon how many people must be sustained, their level of consumption, and the kind of technology used to extract from the Earth and recycle what is needed. These attributes will in turn be determined by the attitudes of the people in the coming decades and the kind of governmental systems under which they will exist.

The Alternative of Technological Restraint

Physicist Murray Gell-Mann terms the current circumstance the "continued fix-it" approach, in which pollution, shortages, and resource problems are identified as they become sufficiently conspicuous and then individually dealt with by advanced nations. This approach leads, at best, to an artificial Earth in which all environments are managed by some means or other. Where the "continued fix-it" approach fails to deal effectively with environmental and social problems, hopeless urban areas like Calcutta will result; perhaps our whole world will become buried in its own garbage. Gell-Mann emphasizes that there *is* another alternative—technological restraint.

Large amounts of research and development could be carried out on alternative technologies, with great restraint displayed in deploying these technologies until the environmental impact has been thoughtfully forecast and balanced against alternative means of satisfying economic necessity. Similar concepts of technological assessment have been expressed by environmentalist Gordon MacDonald and indeed have become popular lately even with some in the U.S. Congress.

But along with technological restraint goes the implication of severely limited consumption, especially among the high-consuming, advanced nations. Ecology, like charity, begins at home. The proportion of natural environment to be retained within the artificial world of a hundred years from now depends on how much the peoples of the advanced nations value those natural environments and will accept limitations on their standards of living and are willing to develop profoundly different life styles.

Environmental Protection—A Question of Values

Technology could reduce the environmental impact of consumption significantly if it were really harnessed to do so. But how much time is required for this social and technological process? The need for low-environmental-impact technology comes at the very time of economic pressures due to genuine resource shortages. Production costs usually must be increased in order to reduce environmental degradation, if only to amortize the costs of new, low-impact technology. Of course, in terms of total cost, including environmental damage and subsequent economic losses, environmental policy may make sound economic sense. But in the short term it often means higher costs in the marketplace. The cost—and value—of protecting the environment, in both economic and human currencies, is a principal political issue of the second half of the twentieth century. It is also a profound question of value, involving dissimilar "primary" values with no common denominator.[4]

The future of natural environments depends on the growth of international world governing. A completely polluted world can be avoided only if the rivalry among the various nations of the world can somehow be contained. To the extent that nations are rivals, from either fear or greed, they will place material consumption above environmental preservation. In a hundred thousand incremental ways, the remaining natural environments will gradually disappear within the lifetime of our children and grandchildren.

ARTIFICIAL PEOPLE?

Man's propensity to modify his natural inheritance points toward an even more unsettling prospect than an artificial planet—artificial people. The requisite scientific knowledge is at hand to permit man consciously to change the genetic makeup of his descendants. Nobel prize-winning geneticist Joshua Lederberg foresees that medical miracles of the future will reflect political priorities more than scientific limitations.

Cloning, the vegetative reproduction of an organism using the genetic makeup of an adult, is in theory applicable even to humans. Most fruit trees now are grown this way from the shoots of mature individuals. Cloning of animals is more difficult than with plants but has been accomplished with a frog. Biologist James Bonner predicts that the first successful cloning of a mammal, a mouse, will be reported within a few years.[5] In some foreseeable future, thousands of infant copies of a particular adult human could be produced by cloning.

An even more science-fiction approach applicable to plants involves the mixing of genes from different species, using fusion within a single cell to produce hybrids. Biologists look forward to the possibility of producing entirely new, more useful plants which combine the best properties of existing ones just as cloning could provide the answer to the cattlemen's dream by making possible the widespread replication of a particularly successful adult animal.

Traditional Practices of Genetic Modification

Man has, in fact, been practicing the modification of his own species in a passive way from earliest times. The caste system in India and codes of marriage among royalty in Europe and elsewhere were positive efforts to influence the genetic makeup of descendants. Exposure of unwanted children in ancient Greece and other societies had a similar effect. The human race has manifested an ugly interest in genocide throughout history as a means of eliminating "inferior populations." Adolf Hitler and the Nazi attempt in World War II to apply the "final solution" to the Jews and Gypsies is but a recent instance in a ghastly series of primitive attempts at genetic engineering.

There has also been an unconscious change in human genetic makeup resulting from the application of modern medicine and technology. The simple existence of eyeglasses is one example in which an intrinsic competitive advantage has been overcome with adequate technology; the occurrence of that deficient gene within the total gene pool of the human race has been enlarged as a result. Diabetes which can be controlled with insulin is another example.

Harrison Brown has pointed out the disquieting implication that such technological compensations for genetic deficiencies are unimportant so long as civilization remains capable of providing the requisite technology. However, should we fall back to the "Things to Come" scenario, among many other unpleasant themes to be encountered would be the sudden recognition of the incapacity of such people to survive in a technologically degenerate society.

Therapeutic Genetic Engineering

Modern medicine has identified many diseases as arising from faulty chromosome makeup, thereby often committing the unfortunate possessor of those chromosomes to a life of misery and his parents or society to enormous financial burden. Hemophilia and Mongolism are well-known cases of this type, and there are many others. Required tests of Rh factor in blood samples of prospective brides and grooms is one societal response. New techniques for testing the unborn fetus for faulty chromosomes are improving to the point where practical and widespread prenatal detection of some genetically abnormal children is imminent. Therapeutic genetic engineering, at least in the industrialized countries, probably will become a reality as the Crunch continues.

But the prospect of even therapeutic genetic engineering carries with it serious echoes and implications. As has been encountered in the recent publicity over sickle-cell anemia among blacks, genetic screening can become a source of significant psychological damage not only to those directly involved but to peripheral groups as well who are unsure whether they can "pass the test." Experience so far suggests to me that psychological problems associated with genetic screening may be more difficult to solve on a practical basis than the medical ones of effective genetic detection and description.

Toward a New Racism?

I distrust the widespread human identification of superiority with one's own group, whether Irish, Italians, Germans, Jews, or Chinese. Often there is a genuine conviction of the superiority of one's own genes—they *must* become the genes of one's children. This is a traditional, inherited view with little objective basis. Yet the time may not be far off when a new kind of racism could develop based on the opportunity for choice by the parents (or state) of the genetic makeup of children.

The basic problem in tampering with human genes is a moral question: *Who decides* which are undesirable? *Who decides?*

Once the idea of influencing the genetic composition of children through therapeutic genetic engineering is accepted, we are but a step away from the difficult choice which biotechnology may be able to offer future parents: the selection of what they consider the ideal genes for their children. In the case of mice and rabbits, mature eggs have already been removed from the ovary of a female of one selected genotype and fertilized in a test tube with the sperm from a male of another selected genotype. The fertilized eggs from the test tube are eventually implanted into the uterus of a selected mother and grow into a normal fetus and thence into a newborn baby. Thus the possibility that future parents may model the genetic makeup of their children on individuals popular in the society around them becomes at least a hypothetical prospect for the future. And again a profound question of value confronts us: Is this process to be voluntary or involuntary?

If voluntary, will we not run the risk of faddism in the selection of the nature of children just as we do in selection of their names? Will we have a whole generation of John Waynes and Raquel Welches on our hands? Will voluntary selection lead to a narrowing of the gene pool and, perhaps unintentionally, development of serious genetic deficiencies as a result?

Involuntary genetic engineering raises (to me) even more chilling questions. An extreme alternative showing how selection could be carried out by society has been discussed by Bonner:

> From each child at birth would be removed a portion of his or her germ cells, and these would then be frozen in the

deep-freeze and kept in dormancy. The child would then be sterilized. The person would live out his or her life and would ultimately die. Some time after his or her death, a review committee would meet and go over the life history of that individual. They would ask the question, "Would we like to have more people like the one here under consideration, or would we not?" If the answer is that we don't want more people like the recently deceased, then we take the germ cells out of the germ bank and throw them away. If the answer is yes, we do want more people like that, then the necessary technical steps are carried through.

There's a lot of logic in [this] suggestion, although it still leaves the thorny problem of how we select the selection committee. Even so, such selective breeding done in an anonymous and farsighted way is not beyond the bounds of possibility.[6]

Bonner seems more concerned with human eugenics than with genetic engineering.

Should Man Try to Go Beyond Himself?

On the other hand, biologist Robert Sinsheimer looks further ahead and considers the creation of totally new kinds of people—genetic engineering in the most innovative manner. Molecular biology has progressed to the point where some can imagine going beyond merely preferential selection from within the existing gene pool (eugenics) to the creation of new, man-made genes. Evolution would then be artificial, no longer simply the product of chance. Sinsheimer argues eloquently that man's memory, intelligence, consciousness, and even the aging of his brain are all attributes capable of enormous improvement.[7] Just as organic chemists were able to create whole new synthetic compounds (plastics) once the molecular structure of natural organic compounds was unraveled early in this century, so may biochemists be able to design synthetic genes for specific attributes once the molecular structure and biological processes of natural genes are fully understood. Sinsheimer advocates genetic *re-engineering* with the aim of developing a greater species, to initiate positive feedback in evolution. The pervasive question of "Who will play God?" reaches its peak with this kind of consideration.

There are objective risks as well as subjective value issues. Mechanistic science has very little understanding of emotion and consciousness—the subjective side of man. Efforts to increase man's capabilities in one aspect, say, memory or intelligence, could unwittingly distort or eliminate subjective aspects of personality simply because we cannot describe them precisely nor understand mechanistically how they arise.

In earlier times, those in the forefront of geographic exploration of this planet often regarded "primitive" peoples as inferior and in need of "improvement." History records repeatedly with a dusty tongue how the smug, self-assured Europeans of the seventeenth, eighteenth, and nineteenth centuries slaughtered into extinction sensitive, valuable peoples. Primitive consciousness was destroyed simply because European man of the time failed to appreciate its peculiar values.

Could an analogous situation arise out of the limited perspective of modern biologists? Modification carries the risk of destroying forever the subjective portion of man.

Genetic Engineering—A Moral Challenge

Regardless of one's personal reaction to the prospects of genetic engineering, it is a dimension of the future that cannot be ignored. Genetic engineering raises profound issues which will have to be faced on both the individual and societal levels. Margaret Mead apparently discounts its importance,[8] while Jacques Cousteau seemingly looks upon genetic engineering as a step toward immortality.[9] A sharp polarization is evident in thoughtful writing: Sinsheimer an articulate advocate, Senator John Tunney a strong opponent, Harrison Brown supporting voluntary efforts. My own view is that man must find within himself the insight and strength necessary to overcome the trials of the Crunch and become a more advanced entity without opening the Pandora's box of genetic reconstitution.

It is most surprising, therefore, that biologist Bonner would offer what I can only describe as an incredible statement, indicating the depths of division that the issue of biological engineering will bring forth:

> ... given the premise that we can in fact better our society, and given the premise that we can avoid devastating war, I conclude that man has in his hands the first rudimentary tools by means of which he can escape extinction and lift our species to a new and better one. *The only remaining question to me, at least, is not a moral or judgmental one, it is a temporal question.* When will we start on this new path?[10] [Italics mine.]

If the morality of abortion and euthanasia can exercise the feelings and beliefs of our society so strongly, then I doubt that many would agree with Bonner that genetic engineering is not a "moral or judgmental" matter. Indeed, it not only strikes at the heart of individual and social morality but carries profound political and philosophical implications as well.

HOMOGENIZATION AND AUTHORITARIANISM

The present is confused by trends toward homogenization and strong countertrends toward diversity.

Accompanying the dislocation of traditional patterns of family and social life has been an almost world-wide increase in crime and other manifestations of disorder. Simultaneously there has also been a sharp increase in centralization of authority, with strong tendencies toward the elimination of deviant, eccentric, and outspoken individuals within many societies.

There are powerful trends in the modern world to winnow out the more extreme personalities and focus toward a more homogeneous blend best suited for living under crowded conditions within large bureaucratic organizations. The "ultimate" solution to the law-and-order problem can be simply to remove the individuality from individuals, a frightening concept but one which cannot be ignored when looking into the future.

Crime and Punishment

The steady increase in crime in the United States has led to an increasing intolerance of certain kinds of "antisocial" behavior and "criminality."[11] Yet modern study of behavioral patterns calls into question the very definition of criminality. Judge David Bazelon was prompted in part by the findings of behavioral science when he wrote the landmark opinion, the *Durham* case, which altered the traditional definition of insanity known as the McNaghten Rules. Under McNaghten a defendant could not be acquitted by reason of insanity unless a mental disorder precluded his knowing right from wrong. In the *Durham* decision, that criterion was replaced by the concept that an accused person is not criminally responsible if his act was the product of a mental disease or defect.

It has become evident over the years that psychiatrists and other social scientists were not ready to accept the responsibilities and commitment to justice that *Durham* both permitted and required of them.[12]

Nevertheless, the insufficiency of the McNaghten Rules continues to disturb many outside the legal and psychiatric professions. Biologist Sinsheimer comments:

> Most crimes of a type considered as insane are performed by people who are not really in control of themselves. They are really mentally ill due to some biochemical or physiological defect. It is probably very difficult for the average human being to even comprehend the kind of stress that such people are under.
>
> So I don't believe they should be punished in the usual sense. I don't think they are acting as free agents. Clearly, of course, they have to be restrained in some manner from committing additional crimes, but that's a different approach to the problem.

Theologian Kelsey is quite definite concerning criminal insanity:

> On this one I can be definite. If an insane person is one who has no control over his actions when he does them, if punishment is effective only when one has control, then punishment of the "insane" criminal is stupid.

Public opinion in the United States, however, seems to be moving toward a more repressive attitude concerning crimes of violence toward others, even while becoming more tolerant of "aberrant" personal acts like homosexuality. In California, recent efforts to restore the death penalty for certain categories of crimes clearly reflect the strong majority opinion of the voters. Of course, within the popular arena there is a blending of inherently distinct concepts concerning punishment of guilt, incarceration of a potential criminal to protect society from future crimes, and the efficacy of unpleasant imprisonment as a deterrent to future crimes. Increased violent crime and the failure so far to find a workable humanitarian ethic beyond the McNaghten Rules reinforce traditional repressive attitudes. This trend leads toward stronger pressures to conform to narrower standards of behavior; when combined with severe punishments to reduce and remove deviant personalities, the net result could be to limit the resultant society to a more homogeneous collection of people.

Is Personality Modification an Alternative?

The tragic confrontation between antisocial behavior and social repression almost demands a humanitarian plea for moderation, for some middle ground. Could moderation lead us to accept personality modification (through psychosurgery, extensive uses of drugs, and perhaps electrical interference with brain processes) as the least inhumane alternative?[13]

Life in many American prisons, or Soviet ones for that matter, remains dehumanizing and horrible. Will the time come when "criminals" would elect to undergo personality modification of some kind in return for freedom?

As the tools of the social scientists become more precise and the capability of predicting criminal behavior in specific individuals is improved, this situation could become a reality. Indeed, some social scientists already call for a conscious policy to remove aggressive instincts from

Homo sapiens. The choice is viewed by some to lie between repression and modification.

In the United States we find it most distressing to learn of the Soviet practice of placing "dissidents" (who, from our point of view, appear entirely reasonable in their requests and demands on their society) in prisons and even in mental institutions to be treated as insane people, perhaps subject to depressant or personality-changing drugs. Yet one can wonder how far from this procedure we may be ourselves in our attempts to deal with law and order. By what objective standard can "antisocial" behavior be judged? Can there ever be a source of authority that can judge challenges to itself?

Toward an Authoritarian America?

Is authoritarian rule in America imminent? Is our majestic experiment with democracy doomed to repeat the rapid transition to totalitarianism exhibited by ancient Greece and Rome? What are the implications of the disparity between material expectations and probable reality for Americans? The prospect of a large middle class that feels it has been denied a fair material reward for dutiful law-abiding life is uncomfortably reminiscent of the circumstances under which European fascism began during the 1930's.

In the United States there has been a relentless growth of national, regional, and local government. Each new economic, environmental, or security crisis further restricts the rights of individuals for the "common good." The Bill of Rights and other fundamental guarantees of democracy are often misunderstood by the very people protected by those rights. The United States has been at war more than at peace for over three decades, which has led to some confusion between the roles of the President and Commander-in-Chief. To many, the Presidency now has assumed a special aura of importance not intended by the Constitution. Indeed, most Presidents from Wilson on seemed to have shared that view. Should the United States become involved in yet another war, for example in the Middle East, the stresses on the constitutional process could be irreversible.

Similarly, if another large depression like that of the thirties were to occur, the chances of an authoritarian regime developing in the United States would be greatly heightened. Indeed, the rapid growth of economic controls and instability in the seventies is unprecedented in peacetime. The balance seems rather precarious—just one more war, just one more depression . . .

The possibility of the United States' becoming a totalitarian state with only the appearance of democratic process has been with us throughout our history. The threat always exists for any democracy should the meaningful process of representation fail and be replaced by a superficial one. Surely the United States' form of governing has changed very greatly in the last half-century. The power of the Executive has increased enormously. The role of the federal Executive, as well as of administrative bodies at the state and local levels, has far more effect on the lives of individual citizens now than in 1920.

Yet at the same time there are encouraging countertrends for those who hope for democracy to succeed. The practical opportunity to vote has been extended not only to women but to blacks and other minority groups, and to the poor. The constituency voting in elections is much more representative now of the actual population than it was in 1920. If we end up in a totalitarian regime, it will more likely be one brought by popular demand, not by the cabal of a minor, unpopular group.

Many Americans were especially troubled by the Watergate scandal because it apparently represented the first widespread use of the powers of the federal government in a conspiracy to conceal wrongdoing by members of that very government. This brings us disturbingly close to the motivation of the KGB in Russia or of the Gestapo in Nazi Germany.

Yet Watergate has been an example of the checks-and-balances system operating. The Executive branch was not successful in its misuse of power (but only because of carelessness in the original break-in), and almost all of the individuals concerned were brought within the jurisdiction of the courts. We are one of the few countries in the world in which such dramatic demonstration of the checking of the power of one branch of government by another is possible. Thus we have survived a major challenge to our democracy, although the total cost of the lapse in both domestic and foreign relationships is yet to be appraised.

Disappearance of the Private Sector

Whether or not America is evolving toward an authoritarian political system, there has been increasing federal influence over the economy throughout most of this century. In the early 1970's America entered into a period of wartime price and wage controls during peacetime. The energy crisis has brought further inroads into the once private management of private enterprise. Individuals managing large corporations own smaller and smaller fractions of the stock; they are primarily managers of production and capital rather than owners of property. Often no single executive feels necessarily responsible for the corporation's role in society, only for satisfying the short-term requirements of his own behavior and balance sheet. In the absence of a corporate "social conscience," government control grows to meet clear-cut social, environmental, and energy crises. Regardless of the political ideology of the Presidency, the independence of the private sector in the United States has steadily declined. In Western Europe the process is much more advanced. In England, for example, government support for universities is almost total; funds are apportioned under the direction of a representative board.

Private institutions are rapidly disappearing. Within only a few more decades, "private" colleges, hospitals, and foundations may well be so dependent upon public funds as no longer to represent an independent aspect of national life. They may still appear to be independent, but they will retain little actual control of operations and policy. The economy of the United States as well as that of other supposedly "free" enterprise countries is becoming more and more managed, and the specter of full national management of the economy cannot be ignored as a plausible future outcome in "capitalist" America.

DIVERSITY, DEMOCRACY, AND DISORDER

There is, however, an alternative point of view. One can make a case for pluralism and argue that diversity is increasing, not diminishing. Indeed, fragmentation seemingly is affecting many industrialized nations.

This phenomenon has been attributed in part to the evolution of technology beyond the mass-produced-single-item stage to the era of enormous diversity of alternative products for the same application.[14] However, more subtle manifestations of technology, especially rapid communication of ideas and propaganda, surely must receive a major share of the credit. Within the United States there has been the rise of black separatism in education. Experiments to break up standardized big-city school systems reflect a movement toward fragmentation and diversification rather than consolidation, cohesiveness, and uniformity. Similarly, television, which in its present form is surely mass communication, is beginning to face the threat of video cassettes and cable television, permitting far more pluralistic communication, entertainment, and education. The total amount and diversity of information continue to rise enormously since the introduction of television to supplant radio after World War II.

More significant to our interest in political situations in society, there is the upwelling militancy of women, policemen, Italians, and Irish in the United States, as well as novel constituencies of hippies, unconventional marriage groups, and changing economic alliances within the country. It has even been asserted that there is a breakdown of the U.S. system of justice in a "litigation explosion." "Ethnicization" is taking place throughout the world. For example, there are separatist movements for French Canadians, renewed pressure within Ireland for independent political entity, and separatist conflicts in Iran (Kurds), Spain (Basques), the Philippines, and Australia, as well as recent bloody civil wars in Nigeria and Sudan. Practically all the governments of Western Europe collapsed during 1973–74, not as part of real change, but mostly as a symptom of their inability to govern effectively.

The Search for Community

Sociologist Nisbet emphasizes that the large bureaucracies of the world are beginning to experience domestic failure.[15] This is manifested in many ways, not the least of which is increasing crime and disorder. The pyramidal bureaucratic governing structure seemingly has become unworkable, especially as it no longer contains a basis for authority derived from some religious or widely held political belief on the part of its constituents. Government no longer is sacred. As a consequence, when authority fails, force must be applied, and the political structures become more and more repressive. Nisbet emphasizes the deep and persistent need of human beings for an association with some "community." This innate need of humans for association with a community is a powerful force in today's society and will be a major factor in how tomorrow's society develops.

The deep need for community can be satisfied only by association and identification; it constitutes a strong force toward social and political diversity, a nucleation process among an otherwise homogeneous population. One must be impressed by the persistent tribal tendencies that are encountered even in such a relatively homogenized country as the United States or the Soviet Union. Similarly, the enduring quality of racial, religious, and ethnic prejudice and animosity, while undesirable attributes, nevertheless help maintain diversity. Emerging nations of Africa and the Middle East are beginning to evidence growing pride in their local cultures. And nationalism is going to remain a potent force in the political rearrangements of at least the near future.

The Prospects for Democracy

Democracy is only meaningful if there are differences in aspiration, values, attitudes, and approach. It must depend upon private institutions, on some system of checks and balances. It is both driven by and is the solution for factions and diverse attitudes. It is the political embodiment of the essence of freedom because real freedom entails the opportunity for genuine choice between alternative actions.[16] Even if alternative actions are permissible in a legal sense in a society, they are meaningless unless there is a diversity of persons to exploit those opportunities. Democracy is threatened on the one hand by authoritarian rule and on the other by the rise in disorder. Democracy is caught in the jaws of a paradoxical history; it needs both diversity and order to flourish.

Toward the Future

Since strong pressures toward both homogenization and diversity, toward both order and disorder, are present in the turbulent world in which we live, how will that balance tilt as the future consumes the present? Rather than try to predict a particular outcome, I shall distinguish three possibilities within the scenarios to be considered in the next two chapters: (1) a continued tendency toward homogenization, leading to a homogeneous people; (2) the survival of diverse natural peoples; and (3) the eventual domination by artificial people. Similarly, in respect to the degree of world governing, I will distinguish between: (1) a strongly centralized world government system and (2) a rather more diffuse kind, similar, for example, to what now exists at the national level in China. In each case I will speculate on the environmental implications. The real trajectory of history lies within the framework of possible outcomes of the present provided by our three-dimensional structure of the future.

VI

THE CRUNCH

*

He wondered again for whom he was writing the diary.
For the future, for the past—for an age that might be
imaginary. And in front of him there lay not death but
annihilation. The diary would be reduced to ashes and
himself to vapor. Only the Thought Police would read
what he had written, before they wiped it out of existence
and out of memory. How could you make appeal to the
future when not a trace of you, not even an anonymous
word scribbled on a piece of paper, could physically survive?

1984[1]

THE CRUNCH IS the unprecedented period in human
history when Earth becomes saturated with humans and
globally unified environmentally and socially. We are already being accelerated through the early phases of the
Crunch. Later, man probably will complete his transition
to a colonial organism, becoming so dependent upon his
fellows as practically to lose the capability for continued
existence as an isolated or scattered family organism. Elements of a new world view, ultimately a new theology,
will be forged in a white-hot crucible of unprecedented
social change as previous bases of human values and behavior fail. It will be a period of truly major social and
cultural evolution for *Homo sapiens* if the "Things to
Come" scenario is bypassed through some effective
means of world governing.

Assuming world conflagration and toxic aqueous and atmospheric conditions are avoided, what other futures are possible? What is the range of possibilities in terms of people, governing systems, and resultant environmental conditions?

The Crunch has come upon us so quickly that it is unlikely the populace of the world could be converted to artificial people through genetic engineering in time to affect the outcome. However, the seeds of a future artificial population could be sown through widespread experimentation. Thus the Crunch can involve only natural people, either heterogeneous peoples like today's or perhaps a more homogeneous population resulting from intense pressures for conformity.

World governing surely must increase if there is to be a future. But will authority be strongly centralized or distributed?

Three distinct scenarios can be developed to illustrate the spectrum of possible outcomes of the Crunch.[2] They are: (1) the Imperial Possibility, diverse peoples governed by a strong, centralized world government; (2) the Superstate Scenario, homogeneous people living under a distributed authoritarian bureaucracy of the advanced nations; and finally (3) a World Confederation, diverse peoples existing in largely autonomous regional "states."

THE IMPERIAL POSSIBILITY

Suppose somebody wins? Or, more likely, suppose somebody backs down? If nationalistic rivalry between the superpowers continues, occasional, sometimes unanticipated, confrontations will develop. But suppose, instead of a stalemate or a delicately executed defusing like the Cuban Missile Crisis, one of the major powers gives in on a basic strategic matter. The stage could be set for gradual world domination by the superpower which won the game of "Nuclear Chicken." Thus could arise the framework of a world empire ruled by one country with one capital, a modern Pax Romana.

Such a hypothetical outcome of the present has profound political, social, and environmental implications. Inasmuch as there would be a single ruling nation, one national source of authority for the entire world, any illusion of egalitarianism for the world's people would rapidly disappear. There would be masters and slaves or at least a social and political hierarchy based on national citizenship. Such an outcome would bode ill for national democracy, which could at most survive in a few small unimportant areas as a local form of self-government.

Cultural and Environmental Diversity

On the other hand, the Imperial system of world governing could preserve much cultural diversity. Indeed, modern emperors, like ancient ones, might well find it desirable to encourage diverse and antagonistic subgroups as a means of ensuring their own continuation in power. Imperial rule also could effectively limit aggression of one state upon another. The only international aggression would be that practiced by the empire upon any substate that defied its rule. Similarly, the need for efficient exploitation and distribution of global economic resources would be met by direct administration. The ruling power could monitor and administer this process, ensuring a high standard of living for its own subjects and arbitrarily low consumption for the remaining world population. Indeed, the underdeveloped nations with already overpopulated conditions presumably would be allowed to suffer the effects of starvation and disease at an accelerated pace in the interest of overall global economy.

The degree of retention of natural environments (versus complete conversion to an artificial earth) probably would reflect to a large extent the prevailing cultural attitudes of the superpower that won. The two current superpowers, the U.S. and the U.S.S.R., evidence relatively high priority for retention of natural areas.

Such a world totalitarian system would have minimal incentive to encourage consumption other than its own. And it would have maximal coercive power and consequent authority to protect natural areas from both pollution and modification. A hypothetical world totalitarian rule (whether the United States were the ruler or ruled) would surely destroy our high degree of individual choice. Yet, ironically, that scenario may include the greatest opportunity for preservation of the world's natural environments.

Is It Possible?

The Imperial Possibility can only be repugnant to those who value their current personal freedoms. It carries with it the horrors of brutal repression of the ruled by the rulers, so dehumanizing a process to both as to make a final mockery of the idealism of Christ, Jefferson, or Marx. Nevertheless, it is useful to inquire: Is such an outcome possible?

It certainly is not impossible. Adolf Hitler and the Nazi aspiration to rule the world were suppressed only three decades ago. The leaders of the U.S. and U.S.S.R. have been vigorously pursuing a genuine détente based upon political equality and parity in strategic weapons. But who can guarantee that one of their successors a decade or two hence will not be tempted to gamble for world supremacy rather than settle for the delicate balance of terror implied by the SALT agreements? American expenditures for armaments have been declining for nearly a decade as a fraction of both gross national product and gross governmental expenditures (including municipal and state expenditures). Yet at the same time the Soviets have been vastly upgrading not only their strategic forces but their conventional ones as well. We are perilously close to that critical point where the Soviets must conspicuously reduce their rate of rearmament, especially those endeavors carrying long-term developmental implications, or the United States will be forced to face the prospect that what is now parity will soon become an unequal relationship between a dominant Soviet military force and a less than adequate American one. Such a disequilibrium between rival superpowers carries with it the pregnant threat of nuclear war as a result of miscalculation. Alternatively, if the unequal partner backs down at a time of confrontation, then the scenario I have labeled the Imperial Possibility plausibly could be the outcome of the present.

Growth of New Ideas

The local diversity tolerable within the Imperial Possibility suggests an interesting implication regarding the growth of new ideas, especially philosophical views relating to fundamental changes in man's view of himself. Philosopher William Irwin Thompson notes the possibility that in the coming social and political turbulence small monastery-like groups of philosophically oriented men may come to exist analogously to the Christian monasteries of the Dark Ages. Even neomysticism conceivably could emerge, aided perhaps by technological aids such as "biofeedback."

A world empire with much diversity at the local level could provide the opportunity for interaction of diverse new insights relating man to his surroundings and to his fellows; even new syntheses might develop. Perhaps there might be an historical analogy between the development during the Roman Empire of the initially underground and eventually official Christian Church and of "monasteries" surviving the Crunch quietly under Imperial rule. Important elements of a future theology could even result, one in which the principles of science must be incorporated successfully into a broader human consciousness.

Emperors eventually tire of subjugating the aspirations of the ruled. The Imperial Possibility could not be an enduring outcome of the present. However, I do believe it to be a possible transitory stage, through the Crunch into the Afterward.

THE SUPERSTATE SCENARIO

Suppose the tendency toward détente continues and a genuine equilibrium emerges, first between the two superpowers and gradually among all advanced nations. What then? One possible outcome would be an interlocking bureaucracy of the advanced nations. In the Superstate there would be no single source of authority. Capitals and sources of authority could be Washington, New York, Moscow, London, Tokyo, Peking, Paris, Cairo, Berlin, and Teheran. There would be no single race of rulers. Rather, they would be Japanese, German, Russian, Chinese, American, English, French, Persian, and Arabian.

They might all dress in the same color suit, carry the same kind of briefcase, sit beside one another on transcontinental jets, and be astonishingly alike in their personalities. Today's corporate personality would become the international personality of the advanced nations. There would be strong tendencies for modification of deviant personalities through both psychological conditioning and physical intervention, including psychosurgery, drugs, and other techniques. Prison and extermination would constitute the "ultimate solution" to remove those chronically guilty of "antisocial behavior." Homogenization will have vanquished disorder if the Superstate scenario develops.

There would be no democracy in such a system. Rather, we would expect a widespread political situation like that discussed in considering the prospect of an authoritarian America. Orwell's *1984* anticipated aspects of the Superstate scenario—perhaps even a plausible initial time scale. However, he wrote at the beginning of the Cold War and couldn't appreciate the possibility, much less the significance, of détente between the U.S. and U.S.S.R.

Pressures Toward Consumption

The natural environment would not fare as well as under the Imperial Possibility, where the philosophy of technological restraint could be imposed by force and consumption would be restrained. Nationalistic competition within the Superstate would be dulled somewhat as a consequence of the balancing of aggressive capabilities of the leading states, yet strong pressure would persist for high consumption among the advanced peoples, with consequent degradation of the world environment. In addition, the very process of arriving at successful environmental agreements would be more complicated. Voluntary participation by at least several of the leading advanced countries would be required in each case.

Protection of certain species of whales from extinction is a timely example. The United States, the Soviet Union, and Japan have been the three principal countries concerned. The United States has terminated its slaughter of whales for food supply. Recently, the Soviet Union accepted some inhibitions. Japan has shown little willingness even to discuss such an agreement. Meanwhile, the slaughter will continue until the slowest member of the triumvirate finally becomes amenable to entering into a binding international agreement limiting further slaughter (or else these remarkable creatures—our big-brained mammal cousins—will become extinct). All of this constitutes an example of Gell-Mann's "fix-it" approach to environmental matters.

However, the Superstate with its distributed bureaucratic authority should be capable generally of avoiding toxic pollution levels through global administration when the threat to well-being is apparent to all the parties concerned. In advanced nations, where there are already national parks and other natural areas, local authority could be free to continue protection of them through domestic regulation.

Is It Possible?

Could it happen? Just as with the Imperial Possibility, it seems to me entirely plausible but not necessarily likely that the Superstate could be the outcome of the present within the next hundred years. There are certainly indications pointing in that direction, including the growing activities of economic cartels, the operation of the International Monetary Fund, and multilateral trade agreements, as well as Soviet-U.S. and Sino-U.S. commercial arrangements. Administrative functions necessarily of international character, dealing with shipping, mail, aviation, radio transmission, and infectious diseases, already exist.

The Nixon-Brezhnev summit meetings to sign strategic-weapons limitation and economic agreements called up a strange image. Both men were dressed alike, and they looked alike. Most importantly, both men said the same kind of things, a major change from only a few years ago. Conceivably détente could portend a genuine growing together of the bureaucracies of the United States and Russia.

Beyond détente, there is an increasing tendency worldwide for governments to emulate large corporations in management procedures and in philosophies. This blending of corporate and governmental structure is the kind of ruling mechanism implied by the Superstate Scenario. There would be a voluntary coalescing of the "establishments" within the advanced countries, especially the technological and managerial elite, to run the world.[3] Philosopher Thompson has called attention to the peculiar character of the modern world that leads us to emulate the characteristics of our enemies and, therefore, grow toward a more homogeneous world.

"We become what we hate" is an old yoga maxim. And in watching the conflict of the Irish Troubles, the Dublin yogi, George William Russell, developed the maxim into a principle of political science: "By intensity of hatred nations create in themselves the characters they imagine in their enemies. Hence it is that all passionate conflicts result in the interchange of characteristics."

If one stops to consider the implications of this principle for the conflicts of the Second World War, he will come to some disquieting conclusions. Japan is now Los Angeles and Detroit, and Big Sur, California, is now a Zen Mountain Center. Germany is now a consumer society and we are the largest militarist state in the history of the world. We have become our enemy.[4]

Hostility to Intellectual Innovation

The Superstate would not afford a healthy environment for the nurturing of underground monasteries or other experimental social arrangements. Pressures for individual homogenization and "normal" behavior would be great, due both to the needs of such a society and to the bureaucratic mentality of those running it.

A contemporary demonstration of the intrinsic enmity of the Superstate toward diversity of thought has been acted out with great courage by dissident Russians like Sakharov and Solzhenitsyn, who have argued forcefully and poignantly that the price of détente should not be U.S. acquiescence in the extermination of minority political or ethnic groups within the Soviet Union.[5] In the Democratic-controlled Congress of the United States, symmetric opposition developed to President Nixon's request for further trade concessions and agreements with the Soviets without concurrent political protection for political and ethnic minorities in the Soviet Union. One of the first acts of the Ford Administration was to attempt to secure such agreements. In both countries, political groups not in power evidently sense the ominous implications for all internal minorities should the détente proceed to a full-scale integration of bureaucracies and unified global authoritarian rule. Diversity anywhere must support diversity everywhere.

The Fate of the Third World

What about the "Have-Not" countries—the under-developed, the developing? What about the Third World? In the Superstate, the main body of coercive power would be in the hands of the bureaucracies of the advanced countries, unencumbered by any widely held philosophical views requiring self-sacrifice to aid those living in the underdeveloped countries. The present disparity in consumption would continue to increase. The poor would be left to suffer in their own misery.

However, the contrast between "Haves" and "Have-Nots" is not entirely synonymous with advanced and underdeveloped countries. Almost invariably, there are poor and oppressed within the advanced countries as well as an affluent ruling elite of some kind in underdeveloped ones. In the Superstate Scenario, the ruling elite of at least some of the underdeveloped countries presumably would become aligned with the Superstate government, as was the case frequently until World War II accelerated the extinction of colonialism and its paternalistic successors. Their function would be to ensure a supply of natural resources, the maintenance of low consumption, and "law and order" in their countries. Under the Superstate Scenario, the Third World, the underdeveloped countries, could be the subject of the most carefully planned and carefully executed world imperialistic scheme yet devised, more thorough even than the national imperialism of the nineteenth century or its more benign twentieth-century descendants.

Yet the Superstate, like the Imperial Possibility, could not be more than a transitory stage during the period of the Crunch. Since it doesn't solve the problem of the

"Have-Nots," it would be subject to terrorism and disruption by extremists. Indeed, the Tupamaros of Uruguay, the MIR of Chile, and ELN of Bolivia with their successful kidnap/ransom acts against government officials and corporation executives may foreshadow new political reality. This Third World balance of terror would pit the futureless urban proletariat, with little resources but even less to lose, against the powerful but vulnerable ruling establishment in a contest of atrocities.

The highly publicized activities of the "Symbionese Liberation Army" represent a naïve attempt to import such techniques to the United States. That effort will fail just as less extreme forms of revolution have failed in the past so long as there is no large disenfranchised proletariat in the United States. Instead, all classes feel threatened by lawless and barbarous political terrorism. In the developing nations of South America, however, with their vast disparity in consumption, different political realities may prevail.

The Superstate must evolve steadily toward complete global homogeneity by assimilation or extermination of the "Have-Nots." Otherwise it would disintegrate into diversity and disorder.

A WORLD CONFEDERATION?

What other possibilities exist? Is there no hope for a future world in which democracy can survive, no alternative to ever greater bureaucracy and supranational totalitarianism?

The only other distinct scenario I find plausible is for the sovereign states of the world to enter voluntarily into extensive world-governing arrangements. Multilateral agreements would be required in order to: (1) limit aggression of one state upon another; (2) provide for mutually acceptable means of distribution of raw materials and manufactured goods; and (3) limit pollution below toxic levels. Unprecedented limitations to sovereignty in international economic, political, and environmental matters would be required; however, there still could be considerable regional autonomy. A great diversity of peoples, cultures, and forms of regional governing could persist through the Crunch under such an arrangement.

The extraordinary intercommunication of the peoples of the world required to develop and maintain this multilateral governing would be a major social experience; profound intellectual and philosophical interactions could be expected as well, perhaps leading to systems of thought and value otherwise unobtainable.

The Price of Diversity

The price of such diversity is clearly one that the advanced nations, the high-consuming countries, would have to pay; the gap between the rich and the poor must narrow. The advanced nations would have to reach agreeable terms with the underdeveloped nations regarding the value of natural resources. As the recent oil negotiations have so dramatically indicated, the Era of Global Shortages has created a seller's market in natural resources. Free market—or producer-oriented cartel—pricing of natural resources means a leveling off or even a reduction of the standard of living in many industrialized countries and an accompanying increase in the gross national income of resource-rich countries.

But why would the advanced countries accept a World Confederation? Altruism and humanitarianism have not sufficed in the past; the pleas of theologians have not been heeded, nor of technologists like Harrison Brown, Roger Revelle, and Glenn Seaborg for the advanced countries to contribute adequately to the development of under-developed countries. The advanced countries might find themselves embracing the World Confederation alternative, despite its negative implications for their standard of living, because the massive bureaucracy implied by either the Imperial Possibility or the Superstate simply didn't work. There may not be any other alternative, except nuclear war and "Things to Come," with its much greater potential reduction of the standard of living for those in the advanced nations.

Just as the Superstate may be the outcome if the balance of history tips in favor of authoritarianism and homogenization, so World Confederation may be the outcome if the balance tilts instead toward fragmentation and diversity.

The Disappearance of Acceptable Authority

Authority in government derives from widely accepted religious or political principles which carry with them implications for individual behavior. In recent centuries such widely accepted principles have collapsed, and Western governments have had to resort more and more to force and coercion. In the Marxist states there has been this pattern also. Certainly the modern history of the Soviet Union would suggest that the principles of Marxism as applied there are no more adequate to provide the authority needed for suitable behavior by its citizens than were those of Czarist times; the constant attention of the KGB and other coercive forces are still required, as well as complete censorship and information suppression. Indeed, the last decade may have been marked by greater repression within the Soviet Union than was the previous one. Marxism, being derived from scientific materialism, carries within it the seeds of its own necessary evolution. It does not provide any source of governmental authority that recognizes the subjective, spiritual side of mankind, no basis for morality beyond material benefit for some "majority" of its recognized citizens.

The future of China is important to the possibility of a World Confederation; she may be too large to be conquered and too persistent culturally to be assimilated by a world Superstate. Her independent survival could help maintain the political and cultural diversity necessary for a World Confederation. Yet China, too, must find a source of governmental authority with a greater life expectancy than Chairman Mao. The "Thoughts of Mao" seem relevant mainly to instituting political and cultural change, rather than providing an enduring framework for a stable society. China needs a "Constitution" and "Bill of Rights" to supplement Mao's "Declaration of Independence."

And what about underdeveloped countries that are also impoverished in natural resources, such as those of sub-Saharan Africa—the newly termed "Fourth World"? Will they be priced out of life itself as a side effect of the economic confrontation between industrialized nations and resource-rich underdeveloped suppliers? If a World Confederation is to develop, then a new sense of responsibility must arise among the newly rich for the traditionally poor. Otherwise, the poor will get poorer as the newly rich get richer, and new forms of terror, disruption, and war must surely result.

The Demise of Natural Environments

What are the environmental implications of a World Confederation? Such an outcome implies genuine participation in world governing by poor, heavily populated nations, nations strongly committed to increase the standard of living of billions if possible, and to avoid in any case catastrophic famine, deprivation, and disease. The World Confederation scenario thus implies high world-wide consumption. There would be neither the political mechanisms nor motivations to withhold natural areas from conversion to man's use, from raising Earth to its maximum bountiful condition.

Furthermore, the World Confederation may come about only as a retreat from a more "organized" international governing system, such as the Superstate or Imperial Possibilities. Thus development of the necessary regulatory agreements and mechanisms to protect endangered species and to avoid pollution may proceed especially slowly. Indeed, such agreements probably would be motivated only by widespread ecological disaster of sufficient visibility to impress large portions of the world's population with the need to avoid even greater future disasters. Political evolution toward a stable means of regulating pollution might proceed just barely ahead of genuine ecological disaster and thus result in less retention of natural environments and natural living entities than even under the Superstate.

The Future of the UN

If there is a role in the world's future for the United Nations, then it will be in the context of a World Confederation. The disappointments, failures, and frequent hypocrisy of the United Nations often have arisen precisely in those situations where powerful nations were willing to apply coercion toward nationalistic objectives. If the rich and powerful nations are less and less able to achieve their objectives through the use of military and economic coercion (as was the tragic lesson of Vietnam), then the pressures of the Crunch could lead them in desperation to accept a more egalitarian relationship among the nations of the world. Therefore the UN should be kept alive and well, because of its potential value in expediting communication and negotiation among a multitude of sovereign nations. It has not been an instrument of international *justice*, nor should we be hopeful that it will become one. The UN can work only when the member nations are motivated by catastrophe or the prospect of it.

The World Confederation alternative is not a Utopian one in which men will act wisely and well merely because they are convinced they should. Rather, it might emerge as the least unsatisfactory means of governing a world racked by widespread social dissatisfaction and by ecological problems of unprecedented magnitude. Nevertheless, it could allow for the maximum diversity of personalities, thought, and political systems through the period of the Crunch, even if it entailed the least diversity of natural environments and wildlife.

FALSE HOPES AND HARD CHOICES

Aren't there any more hopeful prospects for the Crunch? Must the trajectory of history pass among the three dour alternatives listed above, presuming we do avoid "Things to Come"?

Of course, I can't be sure, nor can anyone else. The cultural upheaval and information revolution within which we exist (there are more than thirty thousand books printed and more than a million scientific articles produced per year) preclude even the calm exterior trappings of a scholarly posture, much less precise understanding of what actually is happening on planet Earth.

What other hopes for the future have been evinced? Why aren't they plausible outcomes of the present?

Technological Utopias

A common hope man has held for his future throughout the last century has been that technology can somehow save him. Indeed, present-day Communist philosophy is in effect rooted in that premise. More benign forms of socialism such as Fabian socialism in Britain and the later technocracy movement of the thirties in the United States contained the hope that somehow technocrats, the technological managers, would take control. They would lead us out of the wilderness of chaos and disorder into a Utopian era, or at least to a more stable set of conditions.

However, technically-oriented people are valuable as leaders only if they transcend that background and develop insight into the nature of society and people as well. Unfortunately, the converse is also true; many political leaders of this century would have served their times better had they transcended their humanistic and sometimes myth-oriented backgrounds to deal realistically with quantitative reality in the form of the population explosion, environmental degradation, and related economic implications.

The sometimes sad truth is that desperate times call for greatness in leadership, for unusual attributes of mind and spirit, and that these exist in only limited quantities within the human race. We in America are in conspicuous need of what sociologist Nisbet terms a "Culture Hero," who can combine real wisdom with unusual leadership and popular appeal. Technology can substitute plastic for metal and invent new means of housing, transportation, and agriculture. But it cannot find a substitute for the judgment, wisdom, insight of great leaders.

Nevertheless, the idea of a technologically based Utopian future persists. In 1966 a well-known physicist, John R. Platt, in a book entitled *The Step to Man,* concerned himself with the evolving nature of man and what he may become. He forecasts an eventual plateau in human affairs, similar to what I have identified as the Afterward. He implies this plateau can be reached through wisdom and good will, that the agonies of the Crunch can be avoided if we merely act well and exploit technology rationally. He foresees a greatly reduced work week; population problems have been solved by merely communicating the necessary technology to those affected.

What will we do with our time in that leisured world? Undoubtedly there will be still more travel and more vigorous and daring outdoor recreation. Life will be dull otherwise. Perhaps thousands will climb Everest and millions will ride dolphins. But I think the activities that will really begin to bloom are the creative arts, education, and science. Not just Sunday painting, but Wednesday-Thursday-Friday-Saturday-Sunday painting. Continual rebuilding of your own home to your own taste, filling it with personal ingenuities and bold designs, might become the fashionable thing to do.

One other characteristic of a steady-state world that deserves special mention is its requirement for a high standard of social justice. If we survive at all, after this great disturbing shock-front has faded into a phenomenon of history, it can only be by working out a new attitude of tolerance and mutual support for each other, between colored and white, between rich and poor, between advanced nations and retarded ones. The unemployed, the underprivileged, the underdeveloped, all the groups neglected or exploited by our present arrangements or condemned to exclusion from our prosperity by the accident of parentage or place of birth, form a perpetual seedbed for spokesmen and would-be dictators whose juntas may take over nuclear administration in the name of correcting these wrongs. Our failure to eradicate these evils depresses the standard of living and shortens the probable "half-life" of everyone. *We are now realizing this, in Congress as well as in the councils of the world. What is fortunate for us today is that our new understanding of the educational and developmental basis of prosperity has made it possible and profitable to cure these evils just at the instant when our new weapons technology has made it absolutely necessary to do so.*[6] [Italics mine.]

These words seem even more obsolete than those in Harrison Brown's *The Next Hundred Years.*

The basic idea that somehow technology can solve our problems runs very deep in both Western and Communist worlds. Certainly, technology is a requisite of any future society better than "Things to Come." But there is a basic conflict between maintenance of a high standard of living and leisurely conditions for part of the world and providing the basic necessities of life for billions of potentially starving people in underdeveloped countries. Man is losing the race of rates—population growth versus food production, economic development versus easily available natural resources. Technology isn't likely to produce a magic solution *in time* to relieve man from facing the frightful choices of the Crunch. The hypothetical possibility of a technological Utopia in which the crushing questions of value have been resolved is so distant from the present as to be almost irrelevant.[7]

In the Soviet Union one still senses a naïve belief that automation and the advancement of computing systems are the real keys to Utopia. The United States is more advanced in the deployment of computers and far more familiar with both their advantages and disadvantages.

Few people here feel that society's hopes are enhanced in some way directly because of the existence of complicated computing machines. They have become a necessary part of the world we presently live in, but their effect often has been to dehumanize personal relationships rather than to create a more worthwhile and productive environment for the spirit of man.

Wisdom from the Cosmos?

A sophisticated but equally specious new form of technocracy conceivably could emerge from scientific consideration of the possibility of intelligent life elsewhere in the universe. Many scientists accept such a possibility as plausible, although they consider actual travel between hypothetically inhabited planets very unlikely because of the enormous distances involved. Rather, the interest is in radio or other kinds of communication which might be going on at this very moment. Indeed, personally, I will be disappointed if in my lifetime some positive indication that "We are not alone" is not discovered, perhaps accidentally through astronomical observations.[8]

What I consider to be a false hope is the possibility not only that some evidence of extraterrestrial intelligent life will be discovered but that messages will be received, decoded, and found to contain highly relevant wisdom which when made available to the peoples of the world will significantly affect the outcome of the Crunch. Visionary statements by responsible scientists, like this one, could be misunderstood by desperate people:

> At this very minute, with almost absolute certainty, radio waves sent forth by other intelligent civilizations are falling on the earth. A telescope can be built that, pointed in the right place, and tuned to the right frequency, could discover

these waves. Someday, from somewhere out among the stars, will come the answers to many of the oldest, most important, and most exciting questions mankind has asked.[9]

Thus, through advanced technology, terrestrial mankind would be spared the awesome struggle to acquire its own wisdom. The fallacy in this view arises not only from the unrealistic expectation of quickly finding such a faint signal in the vastness of space and of the electromagnetic spectrum. More seriously, it is quite unlikely that *any* message would be so universally accepted within only a few generations as to override the diverse experiences and consciousness of the world's peoples. In a world in which most inhabitants don't yet realize that the stars seen in the evening are actually other suns, the acceptance of purported extraterrestrial wisdom from the scientific operators of a "Yankee" radio telescope would surely be a slow process, far too slow to change the outcome of the Crunch.[10]

Religious Utopias

Other Utopian views also persist in our culturally telescoped society such as the apocalyptic beliefs of certain religious groups. There is a tendency among the "intelligentsia" to ignore and disregard such groups. But we should not lose sight of the fact that there are millions of Americans—Christian Scientists, Mormons, Jehovah's Witnesses, Seventh-Day Adventists, and Fundamentalist sects—who take issue with widespread compelling evidence of modern geology or modern medical science.[11]

The existence of objective facts which contradict theological doctrine is not a significant factor in the strength of belief of such groups. Astrology is probably more popular in present-day America than ever before—even while the populace is more familiar with science and technology than ever. This phenomenon is part of the irrational reaction to the failure of science and materialism to provide an adequate subjective world for man. The criticism that a particular view is irrational or not logical is quite irrelevant to those whose fundamental orientation is based upon a reaction to such rationalism.

Mystical predictions fueled by frustration and fear can be expected to increase as the crises become more widespread. Apocalyptic and superstitious views of the future may well gather more supporters and hence become a factor in the consciousness of the Crunch.

Back to Nature?

Yet another point of view about the future is encountered frequently in discussions with students: "Back to Nature." Why can't we live peacefully in small communes in a semiagricultural society? Why must we accept urbanization, social pressure, and aggression?

The sad fact is that man has already proceeded much too far into the Crunch—and into the Industrial Revolution—to turn back the tides of violence, hunger, and aggression. Communes currently are tolerated within the confines of a country which can defend its resources and territory from the inroads of others. They do not constitute the way to the future for other than an equally small number should there be affluent societies in the future. In addition, they require and accept interrelationships with an advanced technological society in medicine, musical instruments, telecommunications, and, occasionally, drugs. Yet such an advanced technological society could not exist if any significant fraction of its populace chose "Back to Nature." Finally, the necessities of the Crunch surely will make natural environments less and less available, especially those in which small agriculture settlements presently abound.

"Back to Nature" may or may not be a desirable way of life, but it surely is not an option open to more than a tiny number of people and probably only for a short period of time. Nevertheless, continued experimentation with rural communal living (perhaps centered around electronic systems supporting various forms of biofeedback?) could be an important source of diversity in social and philosophical views through the Crunch into the Afterward.

Suffering, Empathy, and Future Reality

Thus I think the trajectory of the future lies among the three primary alternatives delineated earlier in this chapter, if not in the direction of "Things to Come." Mankind must face the crushing moral and value questions represented by those alternatives. Does the Golden Rule apply to the "Have-Nots"? Is environmental preservation important enough to be paid for in terms of starvation elsewhere and reduced consumption at home? Is the humanitarian ethic (or Western culture) bankrupt as a source of social morality?

I can't answer these questions. But I can assert that futurologists have not been successful in including *all* of man in their syntheses. Technologists view future reality without the protection of cultural optimism or fatalism. There can be a need to avoid in their own minds the immediacy of widespread suffering, a tendency to view humanity in abstract terms such as are suitable for computer modeling. It is my impression that some scientists and engineers as young students selected the physical sciences out of an unconscious desire to avoid the complexities—and emotional demands—involved in more social occupations. Perhaps the apparent narrowness of the technologist's attempt to view both the present and the future arises from similar personality traits.

It may well be that man's capacity for suffering is greater even than we had thought—worse than that represented by Hitler and the Nazis and by Genghis Khan and all the other horrors of our past. During the Crunch man's full capacity to suffer may be exercised, leading him either to a shattered facsimile of himself in some robot society or to a socially evolved creature, ready to take the next step upward in his evolutionary spiral.

Suppose persons living at the beginning of this century had been able to anticipate the full horror of World War I, the Great Depression, the civilian massacres in Spain in 1936, in Nanking in 1937, in 1940 in London, in Kiev in 1941, in Cologne and Dresden in 1944, and in Buchenwald, Hiroshima, and Nagasaki in 1945, or the more recent slaughters in Vietnam, Nigeria, and the Sudan. Or the rape of the Earth, oceans, rivers, and air that would take place by 1975. Surely they would have considered the future incomprehensible and without hope. Yet man has survived these and a multitude of other horrors, and grown more numerous. Many now look back upon those times as "the good old days." So may it be with our future, which we must face with the confidence that man *can* overcome, even if he must sometimes live a seemingly pointless, even tragic life through the Crunch.

VII

AFTERWARD

*

"We don't want to change. Every change is a menace to
stability. That's another reason why we're so chary of applying new inventions. Every discovery in pure science is
potentially subversive; even science must sometimes be
treated as a possible enemy. . . . It isn't only art that's
incompatible with happiness; it's also science."

Brave New World[1]

WHAT LIES AFTER the Crunch—assuming man avoids
the nuclear war and ecological catastrophe of "Things to
Come"? All three scenarios are transitory; each would be
expected to evolve into a more permanent form, once
people, societies, and institutions are not so driven by the
ever-accelerating events of the Crunch. What more distant scenarios are possible once the world's population has
been stabilized, once world governing has evolved to
limit nuclear war and global pollution? What can be dis-
cerned dimly in the Afterward?

The outcome of the Crunch forms the initial conditions
for the Afterward. Whether there be diverse people or
homogeneous people, centralized government or dif-
fused government, it is from that point that the social and
cultural evolution into the Afterward will take place.
From the crucible of disorder and distress of the Crunch
man will have developed new views of himself and of his
relationships to others. Many obsolete institutions, social
mores, and customs will have been finally discarded.

Hopefully mankind will have been strong and wise enough to have retained the best of the past, an appreciation of the immensity of human consciousness, of the importance of the spiritual portion of man, together with an optimism and dedication to his true fulfillment.

In the Afterward, societies can begin to exploit systematically, although not necessarily humanely, the fruits of the explosive development of technology which characterized the Crunch. Genetic engineering will no longer be an endeavor limited in application to salamanders and mice in laboratories. It will constitute a genuine option for widespread application to the human race. Biomedicine should have already extended quite significantly the natural span of the human lifetime.

The technology of communications and computers will have grown enormously even over our present age. The cable-TV society will have emerged in which remote communication predominates over physical transportation. Today's "dehumanized" city life may be looked back upon as incredibly intimate and sensual compared to tomorrow's. Yet a new sophistication in personal interaction may emerge once there is time to fashion a technological environment suitable to man's psyche as well as to his body.

The age of robots will have arrived; machines will be able to carry out not merely programmed tasks but adaptive ones requiring independent decision-making. Just as the prospect of genetic engineering will force a final decision as to who, if anyone, will play God for the human race, so the prospect of sophisticated robots and computers will force man to choose whether he will be a partner to or a slave of machines.

Perhaps even immortality will become a credible objective for those willing to abandon their "biological shells"[2] in the coming centuries and millennia. The most likely opportunity appears to be in combination with computers and other robot devices. As man, terminal man, might evolve, his "essence" could be kept sustained in a complex man-machine relationship; his personality, his self, could live indefinitely. Whether this kind of "life" would really be one worth contemplating is another matter, and the consequences for the species of "immortals" is a topic we'd best leave for our successors to deal with. We are at least, however, in sight of immortality. We can conceive of it in scientific rather than fictional terms.

Finally, mankind may perhaps experience its greatest cultural event: extensive communication from, and eventually to, other intelligent civilizations elsewhere in the Galaxy. Thus to the hard-won attitudes developed during the Crunch, and those traditional values and insights of the past which have survived, will be added a third element: the traditional information, attitudes, and unanticipated information constituting our galactic heritage. These three elements, the past, the Crunch, and the galactic heritage, will be synthesized to form the new world view under which mankind will live for a very long period of time. What is not so clear is what kind of man he will be. Will he represent not just an intellectually and technically advanced being but a spiritually and morally advanced one as well?

A BRAVE NEW WORLD?

Huxley's classic novel, published in 1932,[3] still remains the most lucid description of a combination of totally centralized totalitarian world government and completely artificial people. In *Brave New World* there are no longer any natural children or natural births (with the exception of some primitive "savages" kept on an isolated reservation for Huxley's literary purposes). All humans are produced at a biological factory. In the factory the desired attributes are introduced genetically and later reinforced environmentally. The resulting population is organized in a caste system. Each category of persons fulfills a task necessary for society and is at the same time reasonably happy doing so. To make sure they are happy, the totalitarian government uses the tranquilizing drug *"soma,"* as well as enormous amounts of psychological conditioning.

Brave New World represents the total application of science to remove individuality from individuals in varying degrees, depending upon their station within the society. Only the Alpha Double Pluses, including the highest rulers of the world, retain individual choice unmodified by the psychological conditioning effects of bioengineering. However, even they are the product of the factory.

There must surely be a whole spectrum of possible Brave New Worlds in which genetic engineering could be widely practiced, not all of which would be so banal and extreme as the one described by Huxley. Not all artificial people need be so childish and superficial as his. Nevertheless, artificial people would carry the result of man's judgment of what constitutes desirable personalities instead of those which arise from natural processes.

Even hypothetical hybrid societies, in which artificial people are bred to perform the tasks of labor to support the existence of hypothetically sophisticated, enlightened natural people, strike me as improbable. Genetic engineering and the construction of artificial people during the Crunch or shortly thereafter would probably be prompted by the wish to obtain better social control. However highly motivated, genetic engineering before rather than after mankind has achieved peaceful fulfillment in a natural state seems likely to lead ultimately to something similar to Huxley's *Brave New World*. I can imagine it being introduced much later in human history, when most of today's social, political, and personal problems of the human species have been solved. Then an attempt might be made really to exploit the full biological potential of man, carried out as a long-term cultural endeavor. Such an occurrence would be very late in time, not the kind of thing represented by *Brave New World*.

Is *Brave New World* really possible? Well, Huxley himself certainly thought so. In a foreword written in 1950 for one of the innumerable reprintings of the novel,[4] Huxley commented that whereas originally he had placed *Brave New World* in A.D. 2600, "Today it seems quite possible that the horror may be upon us within a single century. That is, if we refrain from blowing ourselves to smithereens in the interval." Thus, like most recent futurists, Huxley acknowledged that he overestimated his time scale.

If there were a dominant superpower during the Crunch (the "Imperial Possibility"), conceivably genetic engineering might be practiced on the subservient peoples of that empire as a means of enhancing the survival and standard of living of the rulers. At least in that case, the question of "Who will play God?" would already be answered politically. On the other hand, the current policies and activities of totalitarian governments in the socialist countries caused Huxley himself to comment on the ease with which a Brave New World might develop from such a society. There the emphasis would be upon the obtaining of social control by the bureaucratic authorities. Genetic engineering could be one of many techniques used to achieve this result. It is even possible that within a World Confederation, in a particular authoritarian nation, genetic engineering might be initiated internally on the less fortunate or less well-represented of its citizens. Or the desire to create a superman, as most recently manifested by the Nazis, might resurrect itself in mankind's breast and show up as an endorsement of genetic engineering. There seems to be a variety of paths by which we may move toward artificial people and therefore in some sense toward a Brave New World.

How about the environment? Of course, if an artificial planet is established during the Crunch, the reconstruction of natural environments will then be the province of paleontologists and paleoecologists. Even if, however, significant natural areas and natural living organisms have survived, I would wonder how much *artificial* people would value *natural* relics of the past? At present, it is only the subjective, intuitive sense of value of our natural world present in natural people that balances a little the enormous pressure to exploit, modify, and necessarily pollute the Earth. If man is genetically reconditioned to be better suited to a crowded, artificial future, I would not be optimistic about how well his subjective, intuitive appreciation of natural entities would survive.

One of the special terrors that Brave New World holds for me is not only that it could mean the extinction of the great mass of our cultural traditions and experiences and insights, and even the appreciation of nature, but that it very well could be a stable endpoint for the evolution of mankind. There would be very little tension or pressure to force mankind to further change. Indeed, this society would be governed almost entirely to the end of removing tension and pressure. Thus, although man might be the beneficiary of a remarkable technology, and his society virtually free of crime and disorder, he would in effect be dead—a living dead, a zombie.[5] If change and challenge are removed, adaptation and progressive evolution will cease. He might just as well have died the death of "Things to Come" in respect to carrying values into the future, of being worthy to join the Community of the Universe.

HOMOGENEITY?

But there may be another pathway to remove the individuality from individuals and thereby create and maintain the perfectly stable, orderly society. This could be an outgrowth of the Superstate. The tendency toward uniformity and similarity among the peoples of the advanced countries might proceed so relentlessly that national and ethnic differences vanished. The result would be a single, very homogeneous world personality for all citizens—the homogeneous state.

Of course, we still have to worry about what happens to the "Have-Nots." Biologist Bonner commented in *The Next Ninety Years*[6] that if the present tendency toward increasing differences between the peoples of the advanced countries and those of the underdeveloped countries continues, those of the advanced countries may come to look upon those of the underdeveloped countries as a separate species. In fact, they may be that by then, having had to adapt to a totally different way of life. The advanced countries would find it in their own interest at some point simply to get rid of the poor peoples of the world, on the grounds that they were a source of disease. Even now illegal immigration from Mexico is a significant demographic and public health problem.[7] How will the United States react to massive human waves of the future as Mexico's race between births and deaths soars to its agonizing climax? Will the country symbolized by the Statue of Liberty be forced to create a lethal iron curtain to keep people out?

Present societal approaches are often humanitarian,

trying to provide medical services, despite language and cultural differences. However, an alternative option for future societies may be to get rid of the diseased groups, to reduce their numbers by one means or another over time until finally there are no such people. Such neo-racism could find fertile soil in authoritarian societies based upon the premise of the homogeneity of their citizens. Thus if the Superstate actually developed during the Crunch, its probable outcome into the Afterward could be homogeneity.

Homogeneity would be similar to Brave New World in many ways. Individuality will have been greatly reduced in order to facilitate the management of a society composed of so many peoples. There might be an accompanying reduction in the capacity for art and other creative enterprises. Yet there would still be a major difference from Brave New World. If genetic engineering has not been widely practiced, the genetic capability for production of diverse peoples at a future stage will still remain a potential, and a cultural appreciation of nature at least a possibility.

However, if that human, subjective potential were not exercised relatively soon, the inheritance of the past—information, attitudes, and feelings—would simply disappear in the modern Dark Ages with less and less hope of a future Renaissance. On some time scale, homogeneity also becomes a robot society and constitutes a benign failure for mankind in attempting to deal with the tremendous challenge of the Crunch.

AN INTERNATIONAL MAGNA CARTA?

Is there no hope for naturalism in the future? Is mankind doomed to what Huxley called in 1950 "one supranational totalitarianism, called into existence by the social chaos resulting from rapid technological progress in general and the atomic revolution in particular and developing under the need for efficiency and stable instability into the welfare tyranny of Utopia"?[8]

The World Confederation possibility during the Crunch is as plausible as either the Superstate or the Imperial Possibility; the condition of the world at the end of the Crunch could be a totally artificial world having suffered serious ecological disasters, but not irrecoverably destructive ones. Multilateral arrangements between more or less sovereign states could by then have limited warfare and stabilized economic distribution and environmental control. In this scenario, world population will have become stable, probably in part from continued famine and deprivation. However, changing social habits and attitudes within the underdeveloped countries (resulting in part from a gradual but perceptible increase in standard of living there) would also contribute to stability. Thus the rate of change of the environment, the economy, and of the number of human beings upon the planet will have slowed to the point where political and institutional evolution once again could begin to keep pace with the contemporary scene.

A natural evolution might be toward an International Magna Carta. In the future scenario, sovereign nations would evolve their multilateral agreements into the negotiated acceptance of a central world administrative body. This central body would regulate global economic and environmental matters and act as an administrative arbiter of political differences between sovereign states. It could not have large-scale coercive powers, however, without itself becoming a totalitarian world government. Rather, the experience of the Crunch must have matured the political attitudes of the leaders of the world. Their instincts for nationalism and rampant competition must have been dulled sufficiently for them to accept the rule of law and negotiation over that of coercion. Hence there would have to be, in this scenario, some kind of world judicial procedure and associated legal systems to codify the multilateral agreements that had grown up through the Crunch. Such a system of world governing would permit the continued diversity of peoples, cultures, and governmental systems so long as they did not commit physical, economic, or environmental aggression upon their neighbors.

Within the concept of the International Magna Carta, genetic engineering might eventually be introduced after long experimentation under the philosophy of technological restraint. On the other hand, it might be outlawed as a destabilizing influence on the world scene.

EXTRATERRESTRIAL CULTURAL INFLUENCES

It is during the Afterward that I foresee mankind finally joining the Community of the Universe. By that time we will have probably come across evidence of extraterrestrial intelligent life by accident or by search; further, we can hope to have decoded the galactic "junk mail" addressed to stellar "Resident." Later yet we can look forward to intentional two-way communication, probably at radio wavelengths, with other intelligent societies, much older than ours and more mature in their accumulated wisdom. Indeed, such communication could be the major cultural enterprise of future societies, hundreds and thousands of years from now.

How can I be so hopeful that "We are not alone"?[9] Why do I look forward to the discovery of some kind of evidence to prove that statement? The basic reason goes back to an assessment of how likely the development of life here on Earth has been, and, secondarily, how many Earth-like planets may presently orbit other stars in the Galaxy and universe. Paleontologists have traced in reverse the evolution of life to very simple plant life forms; blue-green algae have been discovered in rocks more than three billion years old. Records of earlier stages for the formation of life, including the establishment of the first self-replicating molecule in a liquor of prebiologic organic compounds, have not been found; it is unlikely such processes would leave records now available to us in the ancient rocks. However, similar processes have been simulated in the laboratory. As a result there is a degree of confidence that early atmospheric conditions (before the advent of oxygen), combined with natural occurrences of sunlight, lightning, and vulcanism, could have produced amino acids: the building blocks of DNA and of all living matter. Given enough of these building blocks accumulated in pools or other aqueous collections, the great accident in which a self-replicating molecule first formed by chance seems to some of us reasonably probable.

Nevertheless (we are in the domain of trans-science), so far there is only one instance of an Earth, with life, with intelligence. And there are some loose ends. Why should the transition from primate to conscious man have taken place during the geologically uncommon circumstance of an Ice Age? What role has Earth's unstable magnetic field played in the multiplicity of events required for life to have formed and survived here?

Yet, on balance, to many geologists, geochemists, paleontologists, and biologists, the process of life, even including intelligent life like ourselves, does not represent a scientific miracle. It seems to be a rather likely outcome of the physical conditions which prevailed on the Earth shortly after it cooled enough to be a genuine planet, over four billion years ago.

The question of how frequent Earth-like planets may be in the Galaxy can be assessed by astronomical consideration of the number of stars similar to our Sun. This point of view was first raised by Harlow Shapley,[10] who concluded that Earth must not represent a very uncommon circumstance; his reasoning has been retraced periodically.[11]

The Sun is one of several hundred billion stars making up the Milky Way, which itself is one of the few billion galaxies. Presuming that stars similar to the Sun can also develop planets with environmental conditions suitable for the evolution of life, possibly twenty billion stars fall into this category in the Milky Way galaxy alone. Even if the fraction which developed life is very small, there still must be an enormous number of "earths" within our own Galaxy. It is the very immensity of numbers of Sun-like stars, combined with the reasonableness of an understanding of the process by which life started here on Earth, that leads me and many other scientists to accept the intuition that there is probably a Community of the Universe. Intelligent life is perhaps rather common in the universe, and therefore we should look forward to communicating with and joining that community. Indeed, even the conservative National Academy of Sciences has encouraged that view to some extent.[12]

The great uncertainty, of course, is in the density of such life. How far apart are the stars around which orbit planets with intelligent life? Even the most optimistic view holds that they are very far apart; radio waves traveling at the speed of light would take tens of light-years to reach one another. More conservative estimates suggest that the mean distances are hundreds of light-years, perhaps even greater.

The search for life ultimately must be based upon the intuition that intelligent life exists and not upon a precise expectation of its density or, therefore, of the time required for a search to yield positive results. "To justify such an effort which may require billions of dollars and decades of time, we must truly believe that other intelligent life exists and that contact with it would be enormously stimulating and beneficial to mankind."[13]

But if there is intelligent life elsewhere, why not plan to send rockets to look for it? Perhaps they—the "aliens" —have already done so with us, and some of the bizarre stories of flying saucers and little green men really are accurate. What makes direct travel to other stars, and especially habitable stars, extremely unpromising is a consideration of the distances and therefore the times required for such trips. Let us make the optimistic assumption that nuclear fusion has been tamed (this is the Sun's and an H-bomb's source of energy, which, we hope, ultimately will supply the world's energy needs). Further, let us assume that it would be possible to build a rocket and operate it using this principle. It has been estimated that such a vehicle would use at least 33,000 tons of nuclear fuel representing one *million billion* dollars' worth of valuable energy resource. All this would be required to travel just to the nearest star. To discover life, it may be necessary to make ten thousand such sorties. And the round-trip time would be in the neighborhood of ten to a hundred years per sortie. All of this suggests how preposterous such a program of direct exploration of nearby stars is. Similar arguments seemingly would apply to alien societies. Thus direct travel in random search of other intelligent life seems a pointless enterprise at *any* foreseeable point in our future.

Conversely, it is quite clear that radio communication is adequate both to search for and eventually to communi-

cate with inhabited stars at very great distances, anywhere within our Galaxy. Indeed, the largest radar system
in the world, located in a natural hemisphere in Puerto
Rico, is *already* detectable by a similar instrument
located at a distant point in our Galaxy, provided the
aliens knew our frequency and that we were transmitting
to them! One obvious and achievable way for intelligent
societies to communicate with each other and to provide
for interstellar cultural contact, therefore, is with huge
radio-radar systems. Recently, an interstellar communication system labeled "Cyclops" has been proposed with an
initial price tag of perhaps five to fifteen billion dollars to
be expended over fifteen years.[14] The "Cyclops" concept
involves a technically credible plan to search out through
many hundreds of light-years for intentional transmis-
sions, that is, beacons. If such beacons are discovered,
then the system could focus in and carry out high-rate
communications with such societies.

It is important to realize that the "Cyclops" and other
concept proposals are credible on an engineering basis.
And the scientific expectation of making contact with extraterrestrial societies is plausible enough so that some
effort at least should be given serious attention. I would
raise here, though, a profound question for us and for our
descendants in the Afterward. Will we have anything to
say? Will we be worth talking to? Will we have managed
to bring the best of the Past through the horrors of the
Crunch into the Afterward? Will we have synthesized
those ideas and experiences into an advanced consciousness that would qualify us for membership in the Community of the Universe?

If we can put aside some of the skepticism these concepts may initially cause, let us project ourselves hundreds of years and more beyond the Present. Consider,
first, the impact on terrestrial society of the recognition

that we are not alone; then contemplate the significance of actual communication with intelligent societies elsewhere in the universe. Such communication would be the ultimate realization of the need of man for community.

If man develops a sense of community with the universe, he may well develop valuable insights on life in general. Most importantly, he could view his Earth in a different perspective. He could accept a future reality greater than that represented by local adversary relationships between differing groups of people.

That we are not alone, and that we can look forward to communication with alien societies, could be a dominant influence in the new world view; the sense of cosmic community may be combined with the bitter fruits of the Crunch, and with the wisdom and insights of the Past, to form the world view of our successors.

I see a certain analogy between the Crunch we are immersed in now and the condition of man at the end of the last Ice Age. Then man was widely distributed, living in small groups geographically isolated from one another in periods of great environmental change. A few tribes discovered agriculture and began to accumulate excess foods sufficient to permit the development of leisure intellectual and social activities. A few of those societies in turn gained dominance to provide the beginning of civilization—in Sumeria, in Egypt, in the Indo-Gangetic plain, and perhaps elsewhere on Earth. One might ask, "Why did only a few tribes discover agriculture; why did only a few of those discover social organization adequate to capitalize on it? Why were so many destined to live out their cultural life spans as primitive hunter-gatherer tribes living on the fringes of what became civilization, ultimately to be exterminated in the world-wide rise of industrialism?"

We don't know why. Perhaps there were subtle differences in the way the tribes were structured. Perhaps there were genetic differences. Perhaps the role of a few unusual individuals in the successful societies was enough to tilt the balance. But whatever the reason, there was a selection of tribes; some failed or remained in a state of animalism, others evolved through successive steps to where we are now. Analogously, I regard mankind on Earth as being like one of those tribes. The Crunch is analogous to the environmental challenge of the end of the Ice Age. I think it is an open question as to whether we shall succeed in overcoming the Crunch. Will we develop a truly advanced society and join the Community of the Universe in a way analogous to the successful establishment of civilization in the Middle East? Or will we be found wanting in this crucial test and end in a robot phase such as Brave New World or homogeneity or, worse yet, sink back into the barbarism of "Things to Come"?

It really is up to us, the peoples of the world, and especially the peoples of industrialized nations, to effect our own destiny. If we can come to view ourselves as part of the Community of the Universe, to realize that our history may eventually be communicated and considered by many other intelligent societies elsewhere in the universe, then perhaps our steps can be a little more confident, our sacrifices a little more meaningful, and our perspective broad enough to see beyond the horrors and absurdities of the Crunch to the potentialities of the Afterward.

VIII

VIEWPOINT

*

O, Thomas, will a Race one day stand really tall
Across the Void, across the Universe and all?
And measured out with rocket fire,
At last put Adam's finger forth
As on the Sistine Ceiling
And God's great hand come down the other way
To measure Man and find him Good,
And Gift him with Forever's day?
—RAY BRADBURY[1]

AFTER AFTERWARD

But suppose a definitive search finds that we are indeed alone? Suppose the expectations of scientists like myself and others prove unfounded, that the origin of life on Earth has been a miracle—a scientific miracle? In that case, we will have returned full circle to the metaphysical framework of early religions. Once again we might obtain that special feeling of divinity which must be ascribed to the only place in the universe where intelligent life exists. Once again man could occupy the center of the universe, except this time the immensely greater universe discovered by modern astronomy.

On the other hand, if we are not alone and do successfully surmount the trials of the Crunch to participate in our galactic heritage, then, too, we can approach divinity of a different kind. We join a truly cosmic intelligence, becoming a participating part of that intelligence, reaching out toward what might well be described as a modern Heaven. Ultimately, as our capacity to understand and our consciousness expands, we could share the world of God, God in the sense of cosmic understanding and insight. Thus man indeed may reach toward the heavens—if he can make it through the Crunch retaining his capacity for subjective insight, for love, for compassion, and for true greatness.

Some even ask, "What happens when the Sun burns out —some billions of years from now when the Sun has consumed all its elemental fuel and the Earth will be destroyed in the final phases of the Sun's life?" I frankly find that kind of question hardly worth troubling over as we face the realities of the Crunch. Perhaps it might be similar to the situation of poor old Neanderthal Man during the Ice Ages as he tried to deal with changing climatic conditions and competition from *Homo sapiens.* He surely could not have even imagined our situation, our consciousness, or our problems or solutions. I feel the same way about *Homo intelligentius,* our successor at some distant time. He will contemplate the problem of environmental changes in the vicinity of his star in terms we cannot even imagine.

THE FUTURE—WHAT'S IN IT FOR THE PRESENT?

With the disintegration of religious views that have persisted for two thousand years or more, with growing disorder and disunity throughout the world, and with man's inhumanity to man displayed so visibly on television, it is easy to understand why nihilism and confusion may run rampant. Yet we must look beyond the Crunch. We cannot ignore the consequences for those alive today, our own children, as well as for those yet unborn. We must recognize the unique period of history in which we find ourselves. We must try to perceive dimly the enormous potential that man may yet achieve if we are but strong enough, wise enough, and care enough to persevere through the Crunch. We must not limit our reverence solely to life itself, but include the diversity of life and of consciousness as well.

On a broader level, we must recognize that we do indeed live at a unique point in the history of the world. The next three generations will form the template for the next three millennia. Each of us is expendable in a historical sense and will be consumed by events. But we can influence the future. Those of us in the United States live in the most industrialized and powerful nation in the world at this crucial point in the history of all mankind. We probably have more leverage on the future than any previous generation in the history of man, perhaps more than any future generations will have. We are playing out our roles on a brilliantly lit stage and we should, we must, play them well.

We must resist the temptation to work for a material Heaven on Earth to make up for the mythical Heaven we can no longer believe in strongly enough to provide a goal for life. The Heaven we must work for is that of the future, for a community of people which includes and expands those things we value most now—love, expanded consciousness, free intellect, humanism. We will make our own Heaven or Hell here on Earth during the next three generations. We will make the kind of world that our descendants for many millennia afterward must live in.

Are we up to the task? I feel that we are. I am an optimist, not only because I don't find it useful to adopt the opposite point of view but because I feel that the longing for Good within the human spirit can emerge victorious over destructive tendencies. I think there is something fundamental in men that resists the pressures to turn humanity into robots.

THE FUTURE—WHAT CAN AMERICANS DO ABOUT IT?

It is not possible to discuss the difficulties facing mankind without encountering the common question, "What can we do about it?" And that's very difficult to answer. One cannot offer in response to the penetrating question integrated economic, political, and environmental policies or a powerful religious doctrine.

Yet there are a number of actions I can discern as relevant. And I can answer on a different level how I personally feel about the future and about my actions now.

First, to consider the public attitude toward science and toward reason. We live in an age in which both are under great attack and it is fair to ask, "Is there some other approach? Is there some other way?"

My view is that man has come this far by using his brains. He doesn't really have the option to reject reason at this point. A return to nature or to astrology or to fundamental religion is really just a step down the path to failure and eventual barbarism. Man must make it with his intellect *and his spirit* . . . or fail.

Technology is neither good nor bad intrinsically. It must be used wisely by man, but it must be vigorously exploited as part of man's avenue into the future. But to exploit technology, to expand it, is not necessarily to deploy it. We need to develop greater maturity regarding the impact of the deployment of new kinds of technology. Ironically, it has been in weapons developments that technological assessment and sometimes technological restraint have developed first. Many kinds of weapon systems are assessed, developed, tested, but never deployed because they are not really as effective as desired: more recently, they are sometimes considered to be politically destabilizing. Similarly, we must consider the ecological, economic, and social impact of new technologies, new manufacturing processes, new ways to live, before they are automatically produced and made available for public consumption. We must assess total costs, not just manufacturing expenditures.

In a democratic state, technological assessment can be carried out only if the citizens involved understand and appreciate the need and are willing to consider other values besides short-term material consumption. In the long run, citizens of a democracy must become more mature and understanding about the proper role of technology and, more generally, about their role in history if they are to survive as a democracy. Authoritarian America, the Superstate, or other forms of nonparticipatory authority lie in ambush for a citizenry which fails to accept the responsibility of understanding the world in which it lives.

A common theme in recent years has been: "Well, if we can send a man to the moon, we can certainly do A, B, or C." Unfortunately, this has sometimes not been the case, because the Apollo project was a single-valued technological project involving a commitment to carry out a specific physical action by a particular time and did not involve many other constraints or side effects. However, the massive technological endeavor remains a useful option if successfully directed at objectives really pertinent to future needs. We could, I think, focus Apollo-type efforts on mass education, reduction of the environmental burden in manufacturing or resource-extraction techniques, and development of new sources of energy, for example. The trick is to combine the imagination and popular support of Apollo with clear objectives really pertinent to our future.

Too often large organizations rely on ledgers instead of leadership, efficiency rather than enthusiasm, and propaganda in place of participation. If we are to achieve Apollo-type success in applying technology to domestic problems, comparable commitment and imagination will be required. Apollo was a judicious blend of risks and resources—technological, political, financial, and personal. Major achievement on Earth cannot be purchased any cheaper or more safely.

Finally, the U.S. public needs to recognize and accept the quantitative nature of the modern world. The language and concepts of science are an indispensable part of modern education, and we must be educated. We must raise our personal and intellectual standards and expect our students to emulate us. We must aim for students who are both quantitatively fluent, yet genuinely concerned about society and man. Similarly, we must separate fact from fancy, opinion from prejudice, and reality from wishful thinking in viewing both domestic and international affairs. We can lead the world into the future, or we can fail and contribute to the world's failure.

How about the attitude of scientists toward the public? Science has always been an elite society; now science must broaden its concept of itself to place citizenship of the world above scientific loyalty and discipline. The confrontation between elitism and populism dominates the world's citizenry. Scientists should not be (and will not be permitted to be) bystanders much longer in that fundamental political evolution. Scientists must accept the full intellectual challenge of the modern world, not just that part of it, the ahuman or superficial part, subject to quantitative treatment. Science must understand itself and how it relates to the total circumstances of man. Scientists must recognize the limits of science and tolerate, even more, encourage, intellectual development of modern systems of values and ethics that imply a reality broader than scientific materialism. Science must mutate itself beyond the physical to at least admit, if not understand, the nonphysical.

More generally, science must accept the need for a new world view, to recognize that the age of science is ending. Science must be the willing father of a new set of ideas, indeed a new theology.

The scientist must try to rise above the limitations of his past and of his past institutions such as the National Academy of Sciences.[2] He must recognize, just as the humanist lawyers and politicians with whom he associates must recognize, there is no safe place any more. There is no refuge. Disorder and discontent will spread everywhere and we are all bound together in an attempt to solve them. He must not try to seek refuge in superficial middle-class stereotyped views any more than we can permit our political leaders to do so.

On a more general level, I feel that the scientist must try hard to persuade *Homo sapiens* of his problems—especially those of a quantitative nature—and to indicate what he considers to be wise solutions. However, I think the scientist must develop a special kind of discipline to resist the desire to trick or force *Homo sapiens* to follow what some scientists may believe to be correct solutions. *Homo sapiens* will be successful only if he also has a chance to fail. He can become the greater being of which he is capable only if some chances are taken. The patronizing attitude which can lead to scientific hucksterism (even of so noble a concept as the search for extraterrestrial life) is in the long run unwise. The scientist must try to educate, to participate in dialogue, and to accept himself the consequences of society's actions. He must resign himself to that collective fate, not try to avoid it by social elitism or by intellectual (or eventually even political) cabals.

A key to strength in human affairs lies in not being captive to any particular position or objective—to be able to walk away from anything. He is a better husband who can tolerate the thought of divorce, a better father who can accept the inevitable growth of children into independent adults, a better leader who can forgo the vanity of title, and, I believe, a better potential ancestor of a greater species who can also accept the possibility that it may never evolve. We must have not only the hope and confidence for a favorable outcome but the strength to acknowledge the possibility of an unfavorable one.

The consciousness of man is rapidly spreading outward from his own planet to touch the limits of the universe and both the beginnings and endings of time. In other dimensions, it is spreading out to understand beauty, love, value. May that great potential and vast heritage be successful in the next several hundred years. Man, planetary man, finally has arrived. The question is, will he survive to become galactic man?

REFERENCES, NOTES AND
ELABORATIONS

I. QUEST FOR PERSPECTIVE

1. J. L. Heilbron, *H. G. J. Moseley: The Life and Letters of an English Physicist, 1887–1915* (Berkeley and Los Angeles: University of California Press, 1974), pp. 251–252.
2. Ray Bradbury *et al.*, *Mars and the Mind of Man* (New York: Harper & Row, 1973).
3. Margaret Mead, "Our Open-Ended Future" (from "The Next Billion Years" lecture series, sponsored by NASA/Ames Research Center, Mountain View, California, and UCLA Extension. Lecture presented 1973. Summary published August, 1974, by NASA/Ames Research Center, Moffett Field, California, 94035).
4. Jacques Cousteau, "An Artificial Ocean for an Artificial Planet" (from "The Next Billion Years" lecture series, *op. cit.*). Cousteau said:

   "The main problem is that, in view of the political immaturity abroad today, it is unlikely that mankind will earn survival without a major disaster. If we are more realistically optimistic, we can envisage that in the next 200 years the oceans will be a disaster— today even the remotest beach has patches of oil on it—the continents will be devastated and only 100 million human beings will still be around on Earth. The main terrestrial life form will be insects.

   "All that the humans will have left to them will be their technology and their science. These they will have to use to take on the task of purifying the planet, its oceans and its atmosphere. Race and national concepts will have completely vanished so this rebuilding will then be possible."
5. Paul Ehrlich, *Human Ecology* (San Francisco: W. H. Freeman & Co., 1973).
6. Remarks and comments about the eight authorities cited included the following by one reader of an early draft:

"A rather narrow perspective for judging the human race: eight white, established, middle-class, professional American males. I would also have sought the opinions of people like, for example, Shirley Chisholm, Cesar Chavez, Eqbal Ahmad, President Julius Nyerere of Tanzania, Elaine Morgan, and, of course, ordinary people in many countries."

7. Herman Kahn, *On Thermonuclear War* (Princeton, N.J.: Princeton University Press, 1960).
8. Donella H. Meadows *et al., The Limits to Growth* (New York: Universe Books, 1972).
9. Daniel Bell, *The Coming of the Post-Industrial Society* (New York: Basic Books, 1973).
10. Herman Kahn and Anthony J. Wiener, *The Year 2000* (New York: Macmillan Co., 1967).
11. William Irwin Thompson, quoted in *Time* magazine, August 21, 1972.
12. Harrison Brown, "Herman Cohn in Retrospect," *The Futurist,* September, 1971.

II. SCIENCE AND THE MIND OF MAN

1. From the poem "Etruscan Cypresses," *Complete Poems of D. H. Lawrence,* ed. by Vivian De Sola Pinto and F. Warren Roberts (New York: Viking Press, 1964).
2. (Tasaday Tribe) "Philippine Tribe Said to Live in Caves," *New York Times,* March 27, 1972, p. 6. See also: K. MacLeish and J. Laundis, "Stone-Age Cavemen of the Philippines," *National Geographic, 142,* 2 (1972), pp. 218–249.
3. "Castro Admits Bending Marxism to Fit Cuba," Los Angeles *Times,* January 14, 1974, Pt. I, p. 8.
4. J. William Schopf, "Evolution of the Earth's Biosphere" (from "The Next Billion Years" lecture series, *op. cit.*).
5. Older civilizations and contemporary primitive cultures have an average span of fifteen years per "generation." However, modern advanced cultures have periods approaching twenty years per "generation."
6. Richard E. Leakey, "Skull 1470: New Clue to Earliest Man?," *National Geographic, 143,* 6 (1973), pp. 819–829. See also news item, "Three Million Year Old Bones of Man Found," Los Angeles *Times,* January 14, 1974, Pt. I, p. 5, and also reported elsewhere.
7. Wallace Broecker, "History of Climate," *Geology Today* (Del Mar,

Calif.: CRM Books, 1973), Chapter 17, pp. 433–451.

8. H. H. Lamb, *The Changing Climate* (London: Methuen & Co., Ltd., 1966), pp. 6–7.

9. George J. Kukla and Helena J. Kukla, "Increased Surface Albedo in the Northern Hemisphere," *Science, 183,* 4126 (February 22, 1974), pp. 709–714.

10. Don L. Anderson, "The San Andreas Fault," *Continents Adrift: Readings from Scientific American* (San Francisco: W. H. Freeman & Co., 1972).

11. O. L. Bandy and L. Marincovich, Jr., "Rates of Cenozoic Uplift, Baldwin Hills, Los Angeles, California," *Science, 181* (1973), pp. 653–654.

12. Charles Davison, *Great Earthquakes* (London: Thomas Murby & Co., 1936), pp. 54ff.

13. Robert W. Kates *et al.*, "Human Impact of the Managua Earthquake," *Science 182* (1973), pp. 981–990.

14. David R. Enlow, "Helping Hands in Bangladesh," *War on Hunger, 6,* 9 (1972), p. 10. Also reported in *Time,* December 7, 1970, pp. 28–31.

15. Julian Huxley, in the foreword of *The Phenomenon of Man* by Teilhard de Chardin (New York: Harper & Row, 1959), p. 20.

16. Will Durant, *The Story of Civilization* (New York: Simon and Schuster, 1935–1967).

17. Laurens Van Der Post, *The Lost World of the Kalahari* (New York: William Morrow & Co., 1958).

18. Van Der Post, *The Heart of the Hunter* (New York: William Morrow & Co., 1971).

19. Morton T. Kelsey, *Dreams, the Dark Speech of the Spirit* (Garden City, N.Y.: Doubleday & Co., 1968), pp. 46–47.

20. Kelsey, *Encounter with God* (Minneapolis: Bethany Fellowship, Inc., 1972), pp. 57ff.

21. Carl Jung, *Modern Man in Search of a Soul* (New York: Harcourt, Brace & World, 1933), pp. 260–262.

22. See, for instance, J. L. Ginzburg in Carl Sagan, ed., *Communication with Extraterrestrial Intelligence* (Cambridge, Mass.: MIT Press, 1973; hereinafter referred to as *C.E.T.I.*), p. 201.

23. Donald Menzel, *The World of Flying Saucers* (Garden City, N.Y.: Doubleday & Co., 1963).

24. Edward U. Condon, Scientific Director, University of Colorado, *Scientific Study of Unidentified Flying Objects* (New York: Bantam Books, 1969).

25. R. G. Podolny, "The Number of Advanced Galactic Civilizations" *(C.E.T.I., op. cit.),* p. 185.

26. B. C. Murray, "Reopening the Question," a review of Allen Hynek's book, *The UFO Experience* (Chicago: Regnery, 1972), *Science, 177* (1972), pp. 688–689.

27. Nicholas Wade, "Psychical Research: The Incredible in Search of Credibility," *Science, 181* (1973), pp. 138–143.

28. For similar biological problems in a different setting, see: Dennis Chitty, "Problematic Creatures," a review of John Napier's book, *Bigfoot* (New York: Dutton, 1973), *Science, 182* (1973), p. 376.

29. Alan Weinberg, "Science and Trans-Science," *Science, 177,* 4045 (July 21, 1972), p. 211.

30. B. C. Murray, M. E. Davies, and P. K. Eckman, "Planetary Contamination II: Soviet and U. S. Practices and Policies," *Science, 155* (March 24, 1967), pp. 1505–1511.

31. Morton Kelsey, *Healing and Christianity in Ancient Thought and Modern Times* (New York: Harper & Row, 1973).

32. Thomas Kuhn, *The Structure of Scientific Revolutions* (Chicago: University of Chicago Press, 1962).

33. Charles Frankel, "The Nature and Sources of Irrationalism," *Science, 180* (1973), pp. 927–931.

34. Robert Sinsheimer, "The Brain of Pooh: An Essay on the Limits of Mind," *Engineering and Science,* January, 1970.

35. R. W. Sperry, "Science and the Problem of Values," *Perspectives in Biology and Medicine, 16,* 1 (1973), pp. 115–130.

36. Gunther S. Stent, "Prematurity and Uniqueness in Scientific Discovery," *Scientific American, 227,* 6 (December, 1972), pp. 84–93.

37. W. Ross Adey, "Slow Electrical Phenomena in the Central Nervous System," *Neurosciences Research Symposium Summaries, 4,* (Cambridge, Mass.: MIT Press, 1970), pp. 1–104.

III. RUNAWAY WORLD

1. From "I Taught Them All" (Anonymous, 1937), as quoted in "An Untutored View of a Comprehensive Case" by David L. Bazelon (unpublished, 1972).

2. Tomas Frehka, "The Prospects for a Stationary World Population," *Scientific American, 228,* 3 (1973), pp. 15–23.

3. Harrison Brown and James Bonner, *The Next Hundred Years* (New York: Viking Press, 1957).

4. Harrison Brown, *The Next Ninety Years* (Pasadena: Office of Industrial Associates, Caltech, 1967).

5. "Science and the Citizen," *Scientific American*, 227, 3 (1972), pp. 64–65.

6. The population explosion has a number of direct implications for those of us living today as well as for our children and grandchildren. Revelle, in his "Next Billion Years" lecture, points out that not only is average age increasing, but the mortality of men is higher than that of women. Accordingly, there is developing a population over sixty-five projected to consist of women almost two to one. He thus suggests that some social mores very firmly held now in the developed nations may give way under this disproportionate arithmetic. The custom may develop of shared men over sixty-five; the monogamous relationship between men and women associated with the childbearing ages may evolve beyond the age of procreation. He also points out that the ratio of adults to children will be greatly different, suggesting the prospect of shared children, as was characteristic of the early Polynesian culture. A third point he makes for Americans and others living in a corporate world is that rapid advancement as the goal of young people will have to change. There simply will be much lower advancement rates. Men and women will have to derive greater satisfaction from the character of their jobs, in the fashion of ancient craftsmen, rather than from the prospect of each job being primarily a step to another.

Another change in mores which seems likely to emerge as a result of this rapid demographic change, not just in total population but in age distributions within populations, could be an acceptance of the undesirability of prolonging life beyond the point of active consciousness by means of extensive medical effort. This is but one step away from euthanasia itself, which perhaps will become more acceptable. The deep-seated ethic so profound in Western tradition, of the basic value of individual life and its continuation at any cost, may give way to a new ethic which places value on a participating, active life but less value on an inhibited or infirm one. Similarly, the concept of abortion may become more widely accepted. The life of an unborn individual, without consciousness, will in some senses have to be balanced against the diminished life of a living, conscious person. It would seem that the further demise of privacy and the lessened acceptability of eccentric behavior will be difficult to avoid. With more people there simply will be more crowding and a greater prospect of interference with one individual's behavior by others.

7. Nicholas Wade, "World Food Situation: Pessimism Comes Back into Vogue," *Science, 181* (1973), pp. 634–638.

8. Judith Miller, "Genetic Erosion: Crop Plants Threatened by Government Neglect," *Science, 182* (1973), pp. 1231–1233.

9. William Drummond, "Shortage of Fertilizer Perils India Harvest," Los Angeles *Times,* January 19, 1974, Pt. I, p. 18. See also: "Forecast for Record Grain Crops Is Hedged," Los Angeles *Times,* December 17, 1973, Pt. III, p. 16.

10. Paul W. Richards, "The Tropical Rain Forest," *Scientific American, 229,* 6 (1973), pp. 58–67.

11. Daniel H. Janzen, "Tropical Agroecosystems," *Science, 182* (1973), pp. 1212–1218.

12. C. P. Idyll, "The Anchovy Crisis," *Scientific American, 228,* 6 (1973), pp. 22–29. See also *Science, 185* (1974), p. 337.

13. Roger Revelle, "Living Conditions Worsen as Our Numbers Increase," from the *America and Future of Man* series, 1973, Pasadena *Star News,* January 16, 1974, Pt. C, p. 1; Harrison Brown, "An American Renaissance? A Scientist's View of What America Can Be," *Bulletin of the Atomic Scientists,* June, 1972, pp. 7–12; Harrison Brown, "Science, Technology and the Developing Countries," presented to the U.S. House of Representatives Committee of Science and Astronautics, January, 1971; and Glenn Seaborg, "Science, Technology, and Development: A New World Outlook," *Science, 181* (1973), pp. 13–19.

14. Robert Elegant, "China Pushing Tough Drive to Limit Births," Los Angeles *Times,* October 28, 1973, Pt. V, p. 1.

15. "50,000 to 100,000 Toll Seen in Drought Gripping Ethiopia," figures from a UNICEF report as quoted in Los Angeles *Times,* October 29, 1973, Pt. I, p. 1.

16. Philip H. Abelson, "Energy and National Security," *Science, 179,* 4076 (1973), p. 857; Philip H. Abelson, "An Era of Global Scarcity," *Science, 181,* 4097 (1973), p. 303; Philip H. Abelson, "The Urgent Need for Energy Conservation," *Science, 182,* 4110 (1973), p. 337; and Philip H. Abelson, "Increasing World Energy Supplies," *Science, 182,* 4117 (1973), p. 1087.

17. Thornton Bradshaw, in an address to the Caltech Associates, Los Angeles, January 14, 1974, Pasadena *Star News,* January 15, 1974.

18. Meadows *et al., op. cit.*

19. R. Boyd, "World Dynamics: A Note," *Science, 177* (1972), pp. 516–519.

20. C. Starr and R. Rudman, "Parameters of Technological Growth," *Science, 182* (1973), pp. 358–364.
21. There are constant new indicators of global pollution. Antarctic penguins (surely one of nature's true delights) are threatened by man's pollution. It seems that discharge of raw sewage from permanent scientific research stations in Antarctica is reaching toxic proportions (for them). (Los Angeles *Times,* July 15, 1973.) At the same time we learn that man himself conceivably could be threatened with world-wide climatic change if a massive oil spill developed in the Arctic Sea. It is argued that oil, from, say, a tanker accident, would be emulsified and dispersed very widely by natural processes. Eventually the dispersed black oil could lead to greater absorption of sunlight over a large area of the Arctic ice, thereby upsetting what is clearly a very delicate polar heat balance. (W. J. Campbell and S. Martin, "Oil and Ice in the Arctic Ocean, Possible Large-Scale Interactions," *Science, 181* [1973], pp. 56–58.)
22. L. J. Carter, "Alaska Pipeline: Congress Deaf to Environmentalists," *Science, 181* (1973), *181,* p. 326; "Nixon Announces New Energy Plan," Los Angeles *Times,* September 9, 1973, Pt. I, p. 1; "Offshore Oil Dispute Flares Up at Hearing," Los Angeles *Times,* November 18, 1973, Pt. I, p. 24; "Nixon Signs Alaska Pipeline Legislation," Los Angeles *Times,* November 17, 1973, Pt. I, p. 1; and "Standard of Indiana and Gulf Bid $210.3 Million for Oil Shale Tract," Los Angeles *Times,* January 9, 1974, Pt. I, p. 4.
23. Bureau of Labor Statistics, as reported in Los Angeles *Times,* January 23, 1974, Pt. I, pp. 1–2.
24. "Arabs Risk U.S. Public Demand for Use of Force—Schlesinger," Los Angeles *Times,* January 7, 1974, Pt. I, p. 1; "Arabs Angry at Remark of Schlesinger's," Los Angeles *Times,* January 9, 1974, Pt. I.
25. S. von Hoerner, "Number of Advanced Galactic Civilizations" *(C.E.T.I.; op. cit.),* p. 175.
26. *World Armaments and Disarmaments: S.I.P.R.I. Yearbook 1972* (New York: Int. Inst. for Peace and Conflict Res., Humanities Press, 1972).
27. "Arab Summit Talk on Getting A-Bomb Told," Los Angeles *Times,* December 16, 1973, Pt. I, p. 20.
28. ". . . and Weapons," *Science News, 104* (1973), p. 379; M. Getler, "Russ May Have Sent Nuclear Arms to Egypt," Los Angeles *Times,* November 21, 1974, Pt. I, p. 4; *Aviation Week & Space Technology,*

99 (November, 1973), p. 13; and *Ibid., 99* (December, 1973), p. 15.

29. A different point of view is represented, for example, in the foreword of *Jane's Weapons Systems, 1972–1973* (New York: McGraw-Hill, 1972).

30. Robert Gillett, "Nuclear Safeguards: Holes in the Fence," *Science, 182* (1973), pp. 1112–1114.

31. "The Deadly New Weapons," *Time,* October 22, 1973, p. 37; H. Coleman, "Israeli Air Force Decisive in War," *Aviation Week & Space Technology,* December 2, 1973, pp. 18–21; and "U.S. Finds SA-6 to Be Simple, Effective," *ibid.,* p. 22.

32. W. Tuohy, "Major French-Saudi Arabian Deal Will Trade Oil for Arms," Los Angeles *Times,* January 8, 1974, Pt. I, p. 1.

33. H. G. Wells, *The Shape of Things to Come* (New York: Macmillan Co., 1933).

34. *Ibid.,* pp. 33–34.

35. Harrison Brown, "Resource Needs and Demands," an address to the Nobel Foundation Symposium, Stockholm, September, 1969, p. 24.

IV. A FUTURE ELSEWHERE?

1. This doggerel was written as a comment on the paper by Robert Leighton and Bruce Murray, entitled "Behavior of Carbon Dioxide and Other Volatiles on Mars," *Science, 153* (1966), pp. 138–144.

2. Christopher Kraft, in an address to aerospace firms in Los Angeles on October 5, 1973, Pasadena *Star News,* September 6, 1973.

3. For example, in a book entitled *The Human Dilemma* (New York: Brookdale Press, 1971), businessman Herbert Woodward felt compelled to argue that human colonization of other planets is essential for survival of the human race and must be carried out within the next hundred years or so.

4. Ray Bradbury *et al., Mars and the Mind of Man, op. cit.*

5. Carl Sagan, *Planetary Engineering on Mars* (Cornell University: Center for Radiophysics and Space Research, CRSR No. 554, 1972).

6. Joseph Burns and Martin Harwit, "Towards a More Habitable Mars—or—The Coming Martian Spring," *Icarus, 19* (1973), pp. 126–130.

7. Bruce Murray *et al.,* "Planetary Contamination II," *op. cit.*

8. Carl Sagan, "The Planet Venus" *Science, 133* (1961), p. 849.

9. Stephen Dole, *Habitable Planets for Man* (New York: American Elsevier Publishing Co., 1970); I. S. Shklovskii and Carl Sagan,

Intelligent Life in the Universe (San Francisco: Holden-Day, 1966); *C.E.T.I., op. cit.;* and Stanford/NASA/Ames Research Center, *Project Cyclops* (Publication No. CRII4445, rev. ed., July, 1973).

10. However, to the passengers on a starship, traveling at near the speed of light, units of time take longer to occur. This relativistic phenomenon, called time dilation, allows the travelers to reach their goal within *their* lifetimes, even though time is passing much faster on Earth. Bussard, in his "Galactic Matter and Interstellar Flight" (*Astronautica Acta, 6* [1960], pp. 179–194), proposed an interstellar ramjet using interstellar hydrogen gas as the fuel. This may solve some of the immense problems associated with travel at speeds approaching the speed of light (about 186,000 miles per second), and other propulsion systems have been suggested (*C.E.T.I., op. cit.*, pp. 216–229), but most of the problems of physics and engineering will remain unresolved for some time.

V. DIMENSIONS OF THE FUTURE

1. Aldous Huxley, *Brave New World* (New York: Harper & Row, 1950).

2. Richard Meier, "Designing Resource Conserving Cities" (from "The Next Billion Years" lecture series, *op. cit.*).

3. Jacques Cousteau, "An Artificial Ocean for an Artificial Planet" (from "The Next Billion Years" lecture series, *op. cit.*). A shocking example of oceanic pollution is described by Robert Jones in "New York Horror: Sea of Sludge Lurks Offshore," Los Angeles *Times*, January 8, 1974, Pt. I, p. 1.

4. It is a knotty issue, too, since it involves balancing dissimilar things with no common denominator. I challenged environmentalist Gordon MacDonald on this point in the following dialogue (April, 1973):

MURRAY: You advocate complex "systems" studies to balance apples and oranges? Consider the Alaskan pipeline. We're becoming increasingly dependent on Arabian oil. This has very serious implications internationally in terms of our involvement in the Middle East as well as serious economic implications in terms of outflow of dollars at a time when the dollar is weak. Even a scientist can begin to understand these things at this point. So there is certainly some merit to the argument that there is a value to tapping large resources that are within our own political and economic jurisdiction. The reason not to do this is almost entirely an environmental one. There will be significant environmental damage to an area which is very fragile. Doesn't that mean that somebody has to balance the probable decrement in standard of living for the American public against a certain aesthetic subjective value of protecting the natural environment?

MacDonald: The answer to the final part of this question is Yes. I would disagree with some of the comments that you made leading into the question. I think it is much more than just a balancing of damage to the environment versus dependence on Arabian oil or balance of payments or so forth. There is the longer-term question of how we are to manage our energy resources. Do we want to use those that we control today, or do we want to preserve them for tomorrow? Is it drain America first, or drain America last? So how do you arrive at that decision? I think you arrive at it in several steps. You carry out the kind of scientific, technical analysis that was carried out in the case of the Alaska pipeline to identify, as I think the impact statement has, the danger associated with the pipeline. You also should go through a next step, which unfortunately we didn't go through in the case of the Alaska pipeline. This would be the issuance of the statement that puts forth the technical, scientific, social, and cultural issues for public comment in order to get a variety of views. And, in the end, there should be an up-and-down vote from Congress.

Murray: O.K. What you are describing now is a reasonable mechanism for making a political decision in a democratic way. Still, how can you personally equate a decrement in the standard of living versus preservation of a unique fossil environment left over from the Ice Ages? It is not renewable. Are you asserting there is something other than economics involved? If so, what is the basis of your values? By soliciting popular opinion and voting on it, all you're really doing is just averaging the prejudices and values of the people concerned. I'm asking you, can you apply personally an exterior set of values, or are we just finding a way to compromise the inherited set of values of this particular group of people?

MacDonald: The set of values, of course, is a reflection of our social and cultural traditions. These values may be influenced by the momentary events of today, and the body politic may or may not be the correct body to adjust these values. What is becoming increasingly apparent is that the values one ordinarily associates with the health of society such as GNP are completely inadequate. We have to develop new means of saying whether this society is healthy or not.

MURRAY: We need some values that refer to the aesthetic or spiritual side of the people involved as well.

MACDONALD: I think "aesthetic" and "spiritual" can be considered pejorative terms—terms that carry meanings that are not complete. A person's well-being involves more than how many dollars he can bring in or whether he looks at neon lights or redwoods. There are other aspects. How well can he communicate with other people? What is the societal setting? How does he relate to others?

MURRAY: Let me drive you a little further on this. Suppose the inherited tradition in the United States were not one of appreciation of nature, the value of nature.

MACDONALD: I disagree completely. We don't have a feeling of the value of natural things.

MURRAY: We don't have as much as we should in your mind, but we certainly have some or we wouldn't have any conservation at all.

MACDONALD: Yes, but very different in different places. As an example, I have worked on legislation in three states—New York, New Hampshire, and Vermont. New Hampshire is a state with industry along its southern border, and with forestry or lumbering as its principal industry in the north. Vermont is largely agricultural. At least the eastern part of New York, the Adirondacks, is again a lumbering area. In Vermont, the people develop a feeling of appreciation of land and its values. Vermont now has its Act 250, a far-reaching land-use planning regulatory act. There's no hope of getting that kind of legislation or regulation in New Hampshire because the people there never developed that same feeling.

MURRAY: You have two groups of people here, one of which is more conservation-oriented, and one a more exploitation-oriented group.

MACDONALD: That's an oversimplification.

MURRAY: But my point is that you seem to be passing your own value judgment on which is the more desirable. In other words, you're saying that Vermont's attitude is better, more mature, sophisticated, whatever way you want to call it, compared to New Hampshire's. Is that true?

MACDONALD: It's not a value judgment. It is a recognition that if we're to maintain the ecosystem in which we live, then we must maintain a livable planet. We have to recognize that there are limits to how far we can stress that system. The social well-being of a people depends on the health of their surroundings.

MURRAY: That is still a physical-reality approach. It's economics just translated on a broader scale.

MACDONALD: No, I wouldn't say it is economics translated on a broader scale.

MURRAY: Is there something subjective about that judgment?

MACDONALD: No, no, it's not subjective. It's a recognition that if man as a species is to survive, he must learn how to live in the environment in which he has been placed.

Biologist Sinsheimer, in contrast, evidently doesn't feel *Homo sapiens* must retain natural surroundings in order to survive. He said:

"With respect to preservation of the natural environment versus constructive or economic modification of it, I think that it will be inevitable that there will be no natural environment, if indeed any exists any more. And I am not, philosophically at least, opposed to really large-scale human engineering of the Earth for our own benefit. I only ask that it be done wisely."

5. James Bonner, "Beyond Man's Genetic Lottery" (from "The Next Billion Years" lecture series, *op. cit.*).
6. *Ibid.*
7. Robert Sinsheimer, "Biology and the Future of Man," *Engineering and Science*, California Institute of Technology, June, 1972, pp. 3–8.
8. Margaret Mead, "Our Open-Ended Future" (from "The Next Billion Years" lecture series, *op. cit.*).
9. Cousteau, *op. cit.*
10. Bonner, *op. cit.*

11. Roland Huntford, "Crime in Utopia: Sweden Faces a Startling Crisis," Los Angeles *Times*, Pt. VI, p. 1, September 9, 1973:

"Crimes of violence rise by about five percent a year. Burglaries and car thefts are so common that the police, manifestly understaffed, write them off. Check frauds are endemic. Juvenile delinquency is about on a par with the United States. Drugs are a problem, with about twenty-five percent of all school children being involved at one time or another, according to official statistics.

"About the only area in which the figures are not noticeably high is in that of premeditated murder. But on the other hand, that murky half-world where violence springs from drunkenness is a problem. Murders, usually with knife or axe while in an alcoholic rage, are so common as hardly to be mentioned in the newspapers. And it is advisable to avoid the subway stations in central Stockholm after 9 P.M."

12. David Bazelon, "The Interface of Law and the Behavioral Sciences," Lowell Institute Lecture, Massachusetts General Hospital, Boston, February 26, 1964; David Bazelon, address at the American Association of Correctional Psychologists Conference, Lake Wales, Florida, January 20, 1972; David Bazelon, "Is the Adversary Process Essential to Due Process in Psychiatry?," address to the Joint Meeting of the Cleveland Bar Association and the Cleveland Psychiatric Society, Cleveland, Ohio, October 12, 1973; and David Bazelon, "Psychiatrists and the Adversary Process," *Scientific American, 230,* 6 (1974), p. 18.

13. Biologist Sinsheimer reasons:

"If order is not derived from internal principles, then it must be imposed externally. I think it is going to, of necessity, impose limitations upon the diversity of personalities that are tolerable. You can simply tolerate more extremes or more eccentrics in a less interactive society. I think we need a great deal more understanding of the kinds of limits of diversity that are permissible in a democratic society."

I would comment personally that democratic societies are more tolerant of diversity than some authoritarian ones.

Judge Bazelon emphasizes the importance of monitoring the societal decision process. Bazelon has criticized the correctional psychologists for their role as superficial salve for the conscience of society in purporting to have prisons act in a correctional way when, in fact, this is rarely the case (address to the American

Association of Correctional Psychologists Conference). He has also written a stinging attack, "Follow the Yellow Brick Road" (President's Address, 47th Annual Meeting, American Orthopsychiatric Association, March 23, 1970), on the social scientists who purport to have solutions for today's problems when, in fact, they may not really have any solution for the problems with which society is really concerned.

14. Alvin Toffler, "Future of Law and Order," *Encounter*, 41, 1 (1973), pp. 13–23.

15. Robert A. Nisbet, *The Quest for Community* (New York: Oxford University Press, 1953); and Robert Nisbet, *The Social Philosophers* (New York: Crowell Publishing Co., 1973).

16. Allen Wheelis, *The Moralist* (New York: Basic Books, 1973).

VI. THE CRUNCH

1. George Orwell, *1984* (New York: Harcourt, Brace & World, 1949; authorized reprint published in Signet Classics by the New American Library, 1961), p. 24.

2. A simple combination of the two categories of people with these two degrees of centralization of world government would lead to four rather than three possible scenarios for the Crunch. However, it seems to me unlikely that if a strongly centralized government were to emerge (most likely through dominance by one of the superpowers), it could additionally homogenize the world's peoples in such a short time. Hence I ignore this case.

3. Another development suggestive of the superstate direction of growth is implied by the Club of Rome analysis and report, *The Limits to Growth* (Meadows *et al., op. cit.*). The Club of Rome is a voluntary association of technological elite from several countries who are independently sponsoring a study of the varieties of imminent disaster looming in the period of the Crunch. They are doing so without relationship to or sponsorship by any particular national entity. William Thompson points out that the term "club" suggests a technological elite ready to take over and run society when the disasters of the Crunch become sufficiently compelling. Thompson seems to be suffering from the wounds of technological overexposure at MIT, where he was a professor in the humanities, and accordingly may attach more significance to the Club of Rome than it really warrants.

4. William Irwin Thompson, "We Become What We Hate," *New*

York Times, July 25, 1971, Sect. IV, p. 11.

5. Ernest Conine, "The Soviet Union's Closed Society Affects Us All," Los Angeles *Times,* August 24, 1973, Pt. II, p. 9; Andrei Sakharov, "This, Not That," *New York Times,* September 12, 1973, p. 47; L. J. Carter, "Sakharov: Teetering at the Brink," *Science, 181* (1973), pp. 1228–1231; and Philip Handler, "In the Case of Academician Sakharov, a Plea for 'Free Scholarly Inquiry,'" *NAS/NRC/NAE News Report, 23* (7)(1973), p. 1.

6. John R. Platt, *The Step to Man* (New York: John Wiley & Sons, 1966).

7. With a similarly naïve look into the future, *The Human Dilemma (op. cit.),* businessman Woodward recognized many of the manifestations of the runaway world described in this book also. But his faith in technology is so great that he presumes not only that technology *can* solve these problems but that it will! Indeed, technology will create such a homogeneous Utopian world on Earth that we must begin colonization of other worlds immediately lest we suffer a Darwinian fate resulting from genetic decay due to the static, unchallenging life that man will encounter in his Utopia within a century or so.

8. Obviously such hope is based on personal scientific intuition—trans-science. I am impressed at the rate our detection capability is spreading into the cosmos—a happy by-product of extraordinary advances in infrared, radio, and visible astronomical observing capability. Sagan, in contrast, may evidence less optimism for detection but anticipates a more immediate response should a message be received. To him, "The medium is the message—it means someone has survived the Crunch!"

9. Frank D. Drake (New York: Macmillan Co., *Intelligent Life in Space,* 1967), quoted as preface to *Project Cyclops, op. cit.*

10. One reviewer expresses an interesting alternative view: "Maybe it's the 'Yankee scientific operators' and the institutions supporting them that need the 'purported wisdom' more than the rest of the world's inhabitants."

11. The rites of exorcism were even performed by Roman Catholic priests recently, apparently with at least tacit approval of the Archdiocese of San Francisco, *Newsweek,* February 11, 1974, pp. 66–67.

VII. AFTERWARD

1. Aldous Huxley, *op. cit.*
2. M. Minsky, in "Lifetimes of Technical Civilizations" *(C.E.T.I., op. cit.)*, p. 160.
3. Huxley, *op. cit.*
4. Huxley, *op. cit.*, 1950 edition.
5. Sagan notes also that man might be unable to adapt to an unexpected external catastrophe.
6. Harrison Brown, *The Next Ninety Years, op. cit.*
7. Mike Goodman, "Epidemics a Barrio Specter; TB, Typhoid, Hepatitis Linked to Illegal Immigrants," Los Angeles *Times,* September 16, 1973, Pt. II, p. 1.
8. Huxley, *op. cit.*, 1950 edition, foreword.
9. Walter Sullivan, *We Are Not Alone* (New York: McGraw-Hill, 1964).
10. Harlow Shapley, *Of Stars and Men* (Boston: Beacon Press, 1958).
11. Shklovskii and Sagan, *Intelligent Life in the Universe, op. cit.; C.E.T.I., op. cit.;* and NASA/Ames, *Project Cyclops, op. cit.*
12. National Research Council Astronomy Survey Committee, *Astronomy and Astrophysics for the 70's* (Washington, D.C.: NAS, 1972), pp. 51–52.
13. NASA/Ames, *Project Cyclops, op. cit.*
14. *Ibid.*

VIII. VIEWPOINT

1. Ray Bradbury, *When Elephants Last in the Dooryard Bloomed* (New York: Alfred A. Knopf, 1973), p. 142.
2. The National Academy of Sciences, the College of Cardinals, and the United States Supreme Court are among the only major institutions in the world with no age limit for participating membership. In the case of the National Academy of Sciences, at least, the effect has been to buttress attitudes formed many decades past and, therefore, inhibit the capability for new initiatives for current problems.

Acknowledgments

In addition to the eight persons acknowledged in the Foreword, a large number of others also critically read the many early drafts and offered helpful advice and good suggestions, thus leavening and winnowing the final product. I wish to express appreciation to: Professor Ross Adey, UCLA; Dr. Harold Brown, Caltech; Eric Burgess, freelance science writer; Merton Davies, Rand Corporation; Professor John Guest, University of London; Professor Daniel Kevles, Caltech; Dr. Bernard Oliver, Hewlett-Packard Corporation; Professor Robert Oliver, Caltech; Professor Carl Sagan, Cornell University; Professor Robert Sharp, Caltech; Robert Strom, University of Arizona; John Wilhelm, then of *Time* magazine; and Caltech students Kelly Beatty and James Ogg.

Participation in "The Next Billion Years" lecture series (ably organized by Edwin Duckworth of the NASA/Ames Research Center) in September, 1973, provided a stimulating and timely opportunity to try out in preliminary form some of the ideas developed further in the present book.

Extensive review of early drafts necessarily leads to a large number of successive versions of the MS, a fact best known to Lorna Griffith, who prepared them. I am indebted not only to her skill but to her patience and cheerfulness as well.

Most of us grow steadily away from our parents with the passage of time. Happily, I recently re-encountered my own father, through his responses and suggestions while this book was in preparation, a communication (mainly postal) which has been a beautiful by-product of the endeavor.

To dream, to synthesize, to comment on the present in terms of the future and the past has been good medicine for my own "pervasive anxiety" about spaceship Earth and its crew and passengers. Without the initial and unfailing encouragement of Frances Lindley of Harper & Row, I should have missed entirely the challenge and satisfaction of sharing my own blinding visions and lonely nightmares of this inquiry into the collective fantasies of the future.